MOCHE FINELINE PAINTING
From San José de Moro

Donna McClelland

Donald McClelland

Christopher B. Donnan

MOCHE FINELINE PAINTING
From San José de Moro

COTSEN INSTITUTE OF ARCHAEOLOGY AT UCLA

Funding for this book was provided by

The Elbridge and Evelyn Stuart Foundation

The Committee on Research of the Academic Senate at UCLA

The Ahmanson Foundation

The Cotsen Institute of Archaeology at UCLA

THE COTSEN INSTITUTE OF ARCHAEOLOGY at UCLA is a research unit at the University of California, Los Angeles that promotes the comprehensive and inter-disciplinary study of the human past. Established in 1973, the Cotsen Institute is a unique resource that provides an opportunity for faculty, staff, graduate students, research associates, volunteers and the general public to gather together in their explorations of ancient human societies.

Former President and CEO of Neutrogena Corporation Lloyd E. Cotsen has been associated with UCLA for more than 30 years as a volunteer and donor and maintains a special interest in archaeology. Lloyd E. Cotsen has been an advisor and supporter of the Institute since 1980. In 1999, The UCLA Institute of Archaeology changed its name to the Cotsen Institute of Archaeology at UCLA to honor the longtime support of Lloyd E. Cotsen.

Cotsen Institute Publications specializes in producing high-quality data monographs in several different series, including Monumenta Archaeologica, Monographs, and Perspectives in California Archaeology, as well as innovative ideas in the Cotsen Advanced Seminar Series and the Ideas, Debates and Perspectives Series. Through the generosity of Lloyd E. Cotsen, our publications are subsidized, producing superb volumes at an affordable price.

The Cotsen Institute of Archaeology at UCLA
A163 Fowler
UCLA
Los Angeles, California 90095-1510

Requests for permission to reproduce material from this work should be sent to the Cotsen Institute of Archaeology at the above address.

Printed and bound in Hong Kong by South Sea International Press Ltd.

COVER *Moche Phase V stirrup spout bottle illustrating elements of the Sacrifice Ceremony surrounded by animated objects (see figure 3.126). Photograph by Don Cole.*

TITLE PAGE *Moche V stirrup spout bottle illustrating the Bean and Stick Ceremony (see figure 3.72).*

Library of Congress Cataloging-in-Publication Data

McClelland, Donna.
    Moche fineline painting from San José de Moro / Donna McClelland, Donald McClelland, Christopher B. Donnan.
        p. cm. (Monograph series; 58)
    Includes bibliographical references and index.
    ISBN 978-1-931745-38-3 (pbk. : alk. paper) -- ISBN 978-1-931745-39-0 (cloth : alk. paper)
    1. San José de Moro Site (Peru)--Antiquities. 2. Mochica painting. 3. Mochica pottery--Themes, motives. 4. Mochica artists. I. McClelland, Donald. II. Donnan, Christopher B. III. Cotsen Institute of Archaeology at UCLA. IV. Title.

F3430.1.M6M35 2007
738.0985'16--dc22

                                        2007003445

Contents

Preface

THIS VOLUME IS A SUPPLEMENT to the authors' 1999 publication, *Moche Fineline Painting: Its Evolution and Its Artists* (sometimes referred to as MFP in this volume), and presents a continuation of the research elucidated in that volume. We assume that the readers have access to that volume and will be familiar with its contents. Therefore, we will not repeat information of the following types: general information about the Moche, the five-phase chronology of Moche ceramics first proposed in 1948 by Rafael Larco Hoyle, the standard terminology used throughout these two volumes, the history of research in the UCLA Moche Archive, and our method of producing roll-out drawings of Moche fineline paintings.[1]

The 1999 book traced changes in technique, vessel form, subject matter, and artistic canons in Moche fineline paintings through time, using a sample of more than 2,300 fineline painted vessels. Since over 90 percent of that sample had no provenience, we were generally unable to study the ceramic traditions at individual sites or to define differences between sites. One exception, however, was the site of San José de Moro (hereafter frequently referred to as Moro), located in the lower Jequetepeque Valley. Over many years, we have identified and photographed more than 250 fineline painted ceramic vessels from Moro. Although sculptural, low-relief, and undecorated ceramics have been found in profusion at Moro, this volume focuses exclusively on the fineline painted vessels. In it, we describe the form and decoration of Moro painted vessels and explain how they differ from Moche painted vessels from earlier phases and from other locations. We also include the paintings by twelve more artists from Moro that we have identified since MFP was published.

THIS STUDY WAS MADE POSSIBLE by support from the Elbridge and Evelyn Stuart Foundation, the Committee on Research of the Academic Senate at UCLA, the Ahmanson Foundation, and the Cotsen Institute of Archaeology at UCLA.

Many people kindly assisted in various aspects of this research. Of greatest importance were the collectors and museum personnel who allowed us to photograph the Moche ceramics in their collections and to illustrate many of them in this volume. Their patience, goodwill, and enthusiasm for what we were trying to achieve have been extremely helpful. We appreciate the painstaking efforts of Marydee Donnan and Matthew Enger in proofreading the manuscript and making many valuable suggestions. We are particularly grateful to Luis Jaime Castillo, who generously shared the fineline painted ceramics from his ongoing excavations at Moro since 1992. We would also like to thank Herbert Lucas for his continuing support and encouragement of our research.

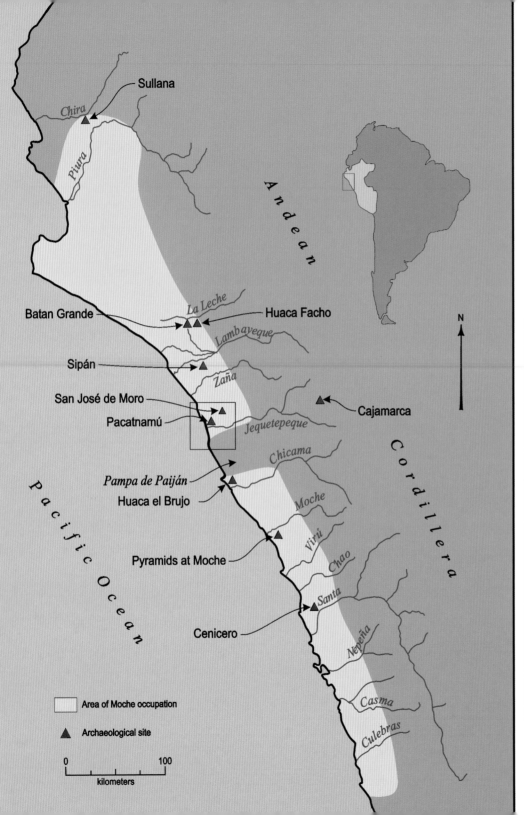

Sullana

Chira

Piura

A n d e a n

1.1   Area of Moche occupation.

La Leche

Batan Grande

Huaca Facho

Lambayeque

Sipán

Zaña

1.2   Lower Jequetepeque Valley.

San José de Moro

Pacatnamú

Jequetepeque

Cajamarca

N

C o r d i l l e r a

Chicama

Pampa de Paiján

Huaca el Brujo

Moche

Virú

Pyramids at Moche

Chao

P a c i f i c   O c e a n

Santa

Cenicero

Negueña

Casma

Culebras

Area of Moche occupation

Archaeological site

0   100
kilometers

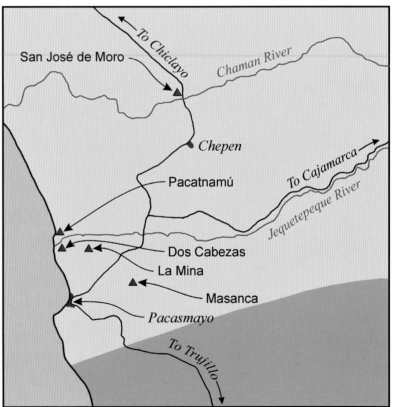

San José de Moro

To Chiclayo

Chaman River

Chepen

Pacatnamú

To Cajamarca

Jequetepeque River

Dos Cabezas

La Mina

Masanca

Pacasmayo

To Trujillo

1 Introduction

MOCHE CIVILIZATION FLOURISHED on the north coast of Peru from A.D. 200 to 800. For many years, archaeologists and art historians viewed the Moche as a single cultural entity, with a ceramic style that evolved through time but was essentially the same throughout the area of its distribution. It was not until the late 1980s that we began to recognize that there was a Northern Moche Region and a Southern Moche Region, each with its own distinct ceramics and its own chronological sequence.[1] The two regions were divided by the Pampa de Paiján, a large expanse of desert that created a natural frontier between them [1.1]. Recognition of the two Moche regions was the first insight that the Moche were not a single monolithic entity but that there were subtle, but discernable, differences in Moche culture between the two large geographic areas. The Northern and Southern Moche Regions are now widely recognized by Moche scholars, and this recognition has been very helpful in reconstructing Moche civilization.

More recently, archaeologists have begun to realize that, although Moche domestic ceramics tend to be similar throughout the area of Moche civilization, the fineware (the elaborately modeled and painted vessels) reflects significant regional and temporal variations. These variations can best be seen as substyles of Moche ceramics. The substyles appear to have been produced by distinct polities as a means of demonstrating their identity. The first substyle to be recognized in a preliminary fashion is the fineline painted ceramics of San José de Moro[2] — the focus of this volume. Another substyle that has been recognized and is in the process of being published was first excavated at the site of La Mina, and has since been found at the sites of Dos Cabezas and Masanca.[3]

1.3 The site of Moro.

The recognition of distinct substyles of Moche ceramics is certain to provide important insight into Moche civilization. To the extent that substyles can be defined and their production identified both geographically and temporally, it will be possible to recognize distinct Moche polities and assess their relative strength as they developed and declined. Furthermore, to the extent that ceramic vessels from one substyle are found in the area of other substyles, it will be possible to assess the degree to which distinct polities were interacting.

The key to this, of course, is having a detailed description of each substyle. The more thorough the description, the easier it will be for scholars to recognize the substyle. The primary objective of this volume is to provide a detailed description of the substyle of San José de Moro, focusing on its distinctive fineline painted vessels.

SAN JOSÉ DE MORO

SAN JOSÉ DE MORO IS LOCATED on the north side of the lower Jequetepeque Valley [1.1, 1.2]. It is adjacent to the Pan-American Highway, the main north-south road that crosses the valley.

The village of San José de Moro covers most of the site today [1.3]. At the time of the Spanish conquest, Moro was an important center of political and religious power, controlling formidable agricultural and maritime resources.[4] Several hundred years earlier, during the late part of the Moche civilization (ca. A.D. 600–800), it contained numerous platforms and architectural complexes and was an important center of artistic and funerary activity.

Looting of tombs at San José de Moro has been occurring for generations. One fineline painted vessel that is almost certainly from Moro was accessioned at the GRASSI Museum für Völkerkunde in Leipzig in 1913 [1.4a], and another entered the collections of the Rhode Island School of Design in 1915 [1.4b]. Fineline painted vessels from Moro continued to appear on the antiquities market over the years. In the 1970s and 1980s, however, there was a dramatic increase in looting at the site, and numerous fineline painted vessels appeared in private collections in Peru. We made every effort to photographically record as many of them as possible and to produce rollout drawings of their paintings. Soon, we began to realize that the vessel forms, the painting style, and the subject matter of the fineline painted vessels from Moro were distinctive. Moreover, since they date to the

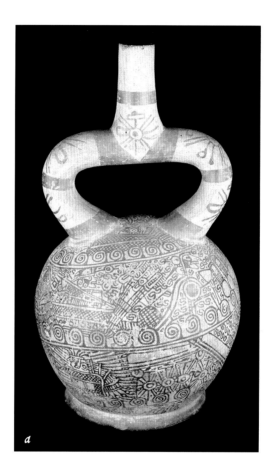 

1.4   Fineline painted vessels looted from Moro in the early twentieth century.[5]

1.5 Room-size tomb containing an elite female and other individuals.

final phase of the Moche and have both valley and site provenience, they provided a unique opportunity to observe a large sample of fineline painted ceramics from a single time and place.

Unfortunately, none of the vessels that we recorded had been excavated archaeologically, and thus we had no way of knowing their original context. We did not know whether they were from male, female, or child burials or whether the interred individuals possessed low or high status. Nor did we know how the tombs were constructed, how many vessels or other objects might be associated in a tomb, or whether the painted vessels buried in a tomb illustrated similar subjects. Realizing that our sample of fineline vessels from Moro would have much more archaeological value if we understood their burial context and associations, we organized an archaeological excavation at Moro in an attempt to find unlooted tombs with fineline painted vessels. Christopher B. Donnan and Luis Jaime Castillo codirected the first two-year excavation project (1991–1992),[6] and since 1992, the excavation has continued under the direction of Luis Jaime Castillo.[7]

The excavations at Moro have yielded numerous burials containing fineline painted ceramics. They are found in simple boot-shaped shaft tombs containing from one to three individuals, as well as in more elaborate room-size tomb chambers containing up to five individuals [1.5]. Although the room-size tombs contain a greater quantity and quality of associated objects than the simpler tombs, fineline painted ceramics are rare in both types. In a room-size tomb containing over 2,100 ceramic vessels, for example, there were only four fineline painted vessels, and the five room-shaped tombs excavated in 1991–1992 contained a total of only nine fineline painted vessels.

The primary individual in each of the two most elaborate room-size tombs was a female. Each tomb contained a large copper mask and copper plumes, as well as a ceramic or copper goblet [1.6]. Our iconographic studies indicate that similar plumes and goblets are associated with elite females.[8] Female figures have roles in several activities painted in fineline at Moro (see Reed Boats, p. 30; Crescent Boats, p. 44; The Burial Theme, p. 96; and The Waved Spiral Narrative, p. 117). These female figures resemble the figures

Copper plumes

Fineline painted vessel illustrating crescent boat (also see figure 4.6 and p. 44)

Ceramic goblet (also see figure 2.10)

Copper goblet

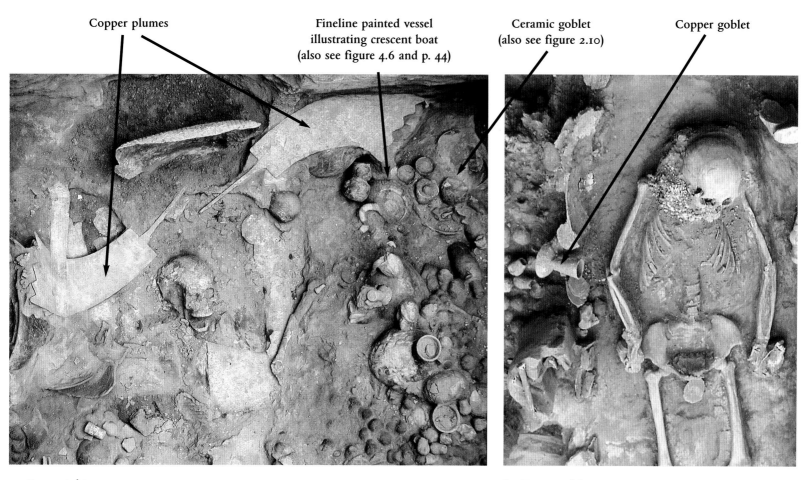

a *Excavated in 1991.*

b *Excavated in 1992.*

1.6 Elite female burials.

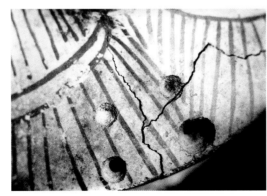

a Heavily abraded Moro vessel.

b Moro stirrup spout vessel that was broken and reworked to create a small bowl before being buried.

c Moro vessel with ancient repair (another view is shown in figure 4.11).

1.7 Damaged vessels from Moro burials.

that we have referred to as the Priestess or Figure C in the Sacrifice Ceremony.[9] However, because of differences in her headdress and clothing, we refer to her generically in this book as the female or elite female. These elaborate tombs indicate that some Moche females held high status in the Moro community.

The painted fineline ceramics found in burials at Moro were not made specifically as burial goods. Nearly all have signs of abrasion, breakage, or repair, indicating that they were used extensively before being placed in tombs [1.7].[10]

MOCHE CERAMIC CHRONOLOGY

IN 1948, RAFAEL LARCO FIRST PROPOSED that Moche ceramics evolved through five sequential phases, Phase I through Phase V.[11] Although these phases have been confirmed repeatedly by subsequent archaeological excavation and art historical analysis,[12] we now realize that Larco's five-phase chronology is valid only for the Southern Moche Region — the valleys south of the Pampa de Paiján. It is in those valleys, however, that the Moche fineline painting tradition began and evolved from Phase I through Phase IV. Production was concentrated largely in the Moche and Chicama valleys, and the painted vessels were distributed in these valleys as well as in the Virú, Chao, and Santa valleys to the south. Thus, both the production and distribution of fineline painted ceramics was largely restricted to the Southern Moche Region.

North of the Pampa de Paiján, in the Northern Moche Region, very few fineline painted ceramics have been found that are earlier than Phase V, and most of those appear to have been produced in the Southern Moche Region. This changed dramatically in Phase V. Although fineline painted vessels continued to be produced in the Southern Moche Region, quantities of fineline painted ceramics also began to be produced in the Northern Moche Region, at the site of San José de Moro.

In order to facilitate comparison between Moro ceramics and ceramics from the Southern Moche Region, we will use Larco's five-phase chronology (Phases I through V) when referring to ceramics of the Southern Moche Region, and Late Moche to refer to the fineline painted ceramics that were produced at San José de Moro during Phase V of Larco's chronology.[13]

THE SAMPLE

WE FIRST BECAME AWARE of the distinctive features of the fineline painted vessels from Moro when we recorded numerous examples that were being looted at the site in the 1970s and 1980s. The source of these vessels was confirmed by finding fragments of fineline painted vessels of this type on the surface of the site of Moro, and learning from the people living in the village that similar vessels were often found in local tombs. Further confirmation has come from more than fifteen years of excavations at the site since 1991; fineline painted vessels with these characteristics have been excavated repeatedly in the burials. Moreover, there is no other location where more than three vessels or sherds with these distinctive features have been reported.

Once the characteristics of fineline painted vessels from San José de Moro were clearly recognized, it became possible to identify in museums and private collections other painted vessels that had no provenience, and to attribute them to Moro. Many of these have been included in the sample presented in this volume.

Our confidence that the vessels in our sample came from Moro varies according to the circumstances under which the vessels became known to us. We have developed the following scale indicating our confidence that a vessel came from Moro (category 1 indicates highest confidence), along with the approximate percentage of vessels in each category in our illustrated sample:

1   The vessel or sherd was excavated at Moro (21 percent).
2   Looters recall finding vessel and could describe its context and/or location at Moro (43 percent).
3   The vessel was painted by an artist who had painted another vessel that was excavated at Moro (5 percent).
4   The vessel was recorded in the hands of dealer or knowledgeable local collector who was confident that it was from Moro (7 percent).
5   No provenience available, but the vessel form and painting style are consistent with known Moro vessels (23 percent).

The confidence level for each vessel is indicated by a numeral from 1 to 5 in square brackets in the Sources of Illustrations list.

The total number of vessels in these five categories is about 255, of which 227 are illustrated in this volume. All vessels in Categories 1 and 2 were found in tombs or caches,[14] and we assume that those in the other categories were as well.

2   Moro-Style Painted Vessels

M OST MORO PAINTINGS are on Moche vessel forms. About one-seventh, however, are on vessel forms derived from Huari. Similarly, although most of the Moro-style fineline painting was executed using traditional Moche red and white slip colors, some paintings were in polychrome slip—a technique derived from Huari.[1]

2.1   Comparison of late Moche stirrup spout bottles from Northern and Southern Moche Regions.

a   Northern (Moro) style.   *b   Southern style.*

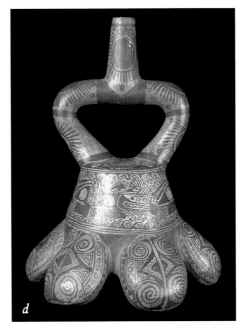

MOCHE VESSEL FORMS

MOST MORO-STYLE FINELINE PAINTED VESSELS are stirrup spout bottles. They differ in several ways from stirrup spout bottles produced in the Southern Moche Region during Phase V [2.1]. Some Moro vessel chambers are spherical [2.2a], but many have curved equators [2.2b] or sharply angled equators dividing the chamber horizontally into two halves [2.2c]. In contrast, many bottles from the Southern Moche Region have flat-bottomed ovoid chambers, a form not found at Moro [2.1b]. Most Moro stirrup spout bottles have ring bases, but ring bases are rare in the Southern Moche Region.

One type of stirrup spout bottle found at Moro has a cylindrical chamber with six lobes symmetrically arranged around its base [2.2d].

2.2 *Chamber forms of Moro stirrup spout bottles.*

A few stirrup spout vessels have a tube passing horizontally or vertically through the chamber [2.3].[2] Others have an enclosed inner chamber within a perforated outer chamber. One has modeled heads peering out through six large circular holes cut through the outer chamber [2.4a]. Another has a chamber within the outer chamber, as well as a spout within the outer spout [2.4b]. Forty-two small holes perforate the outer chamber and outer spout. A third bottle, now missing its spout, has a doughnut-shaped chamber within the outer chamber [2.4c]. Holes on the front and back of the outer chamber align with the center of the doughnut-shaped inner chamber so one can see completely through the vessel's chamber. It would have been possible to fill and empty all three of these vessels through their spouts. Their inner chambers would have been fully functional containers of liquid.

2.3 Stirrup spout bottles with tubes through chambers. Modeled frogs are near the tube opening in figure 2.3a.

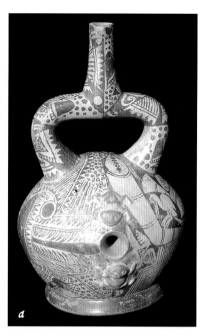

a

b

2.4 Stirrup spout bottles with inner chambers and perforated outer chambers.

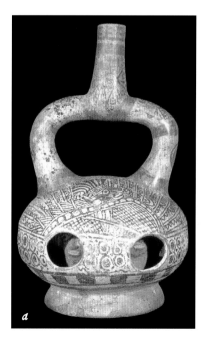

a

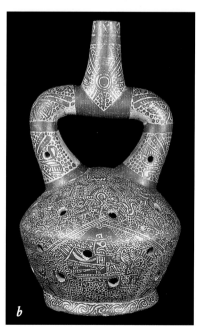

b

c

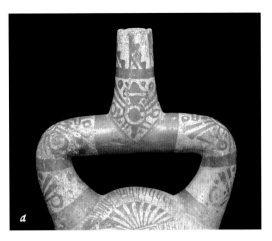

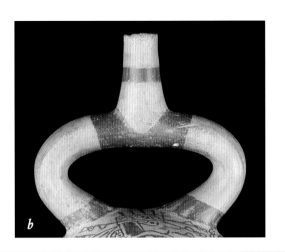

2.5   Moro stirrup spouts. The upper
spout in figure 2.5c has been restored.

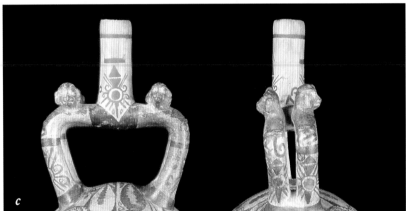

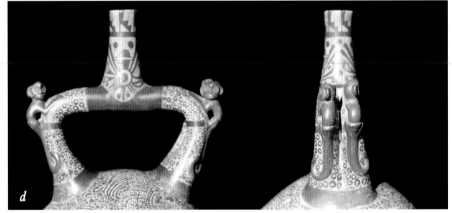

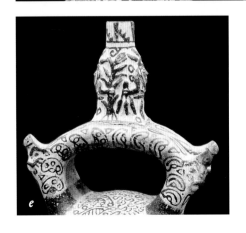

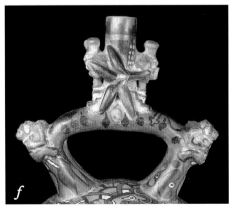

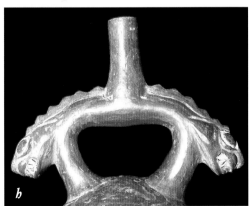

The upper portion of the stirrup spouts from both Moro [2.1a] and the Southern Moche Region [2.1b] taper toward the top, but the arch of Moro stirrup spouts is more widely spaced where it joins the chamber. The arch is often flattened on top, with fairly sharply curved shoulders [2.5a], and the arch is almost always wider than it is high [2.5b]. Moro potters produced some stirrup spouts with double arches and single upper spouts [2.5c–d]. Most of these stirrup spouts have modeled monkeys on the shoulders of the arch [2.5c–d], although a few have modeled frogs [2.5e–f]. The spouts with frogs are thickened and have two modeled standing figures holding plants. These spouts also feature beans painted on the arch. A similar spout lacks the frogs but has the modeled standing figures [2.5g]. One stirrup spout bottle has a double-headed snake modeled on the arch [2.5h].

2.6   Spout and handle bottle.

There is only one spout and handle bottle in our sample, although its spout and handle are missing [2.6]. We have one example of a false jar neck bottle [2.7].

2.7   False jar neck bottle.

A flask-shaped jar with lugs on its shoulders is unique in the Moro sample [2.8]. Several jars with fineline painting have been found at Moro [2.9]. One is a face-neck jar [2.9b]. These bear Moche designs, but also have Huari chevrons around their rims.

2.8 *Flask-shaped jar with crescent boat painting.*

2.9 *Moro jars.*

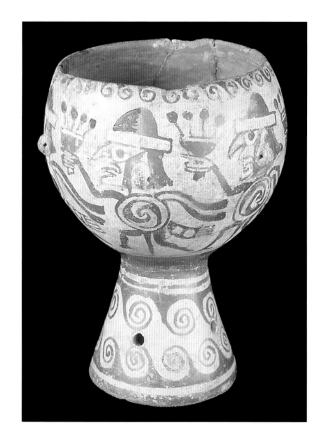

The ceramic goblet in figure 2.10 is the only known Moche goblet with fineline painting. Each figure in the painting is an anthropomorphized club and shield carrying a goblet. The circular objects rising from the goblets may represent blood collected from captive warriors (see The Warrior Narrative, p. 114).

Although a few flaring bowls have been found at Moro, we know of none with fineline painting, nor do we have any confirmed fineline painted dippers.

2.10 Moro ceramic goblet.

2.11 *Double spout and bridge bottle painted with white slip on a red background.*

VESSEL FORMS DERIVED FROM HUARI

SOME OF THE MORO FINELINE PAINTINGS are on double spout and bridge bottles, a vessel form derived from the Huari ceramic tradition [2.11]. The chambers of some double spout and bridge bottles are oblate [2.12a]. Others have chambers with curved equators [2.12b], sharply angled equators [2.12c], or chambers with six symmetrically arranged lobes [2.12d][3] — forms that are similar to the chambers of Moro stirrup spout bottles. The unusual chamber of the double spout and bridge vessel in figure 2.12e appears to be in the form of a gourd or bag constricted, possibly by cords, into eight bulges.[4] None of the double spout and bridge bottles in our sample have ring bases.

a

2.12 Chamber forms of double spout and bridge bottles.

b

c

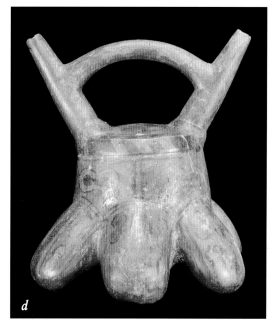

d

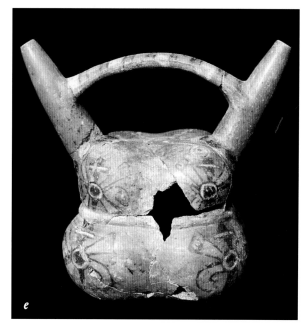

e

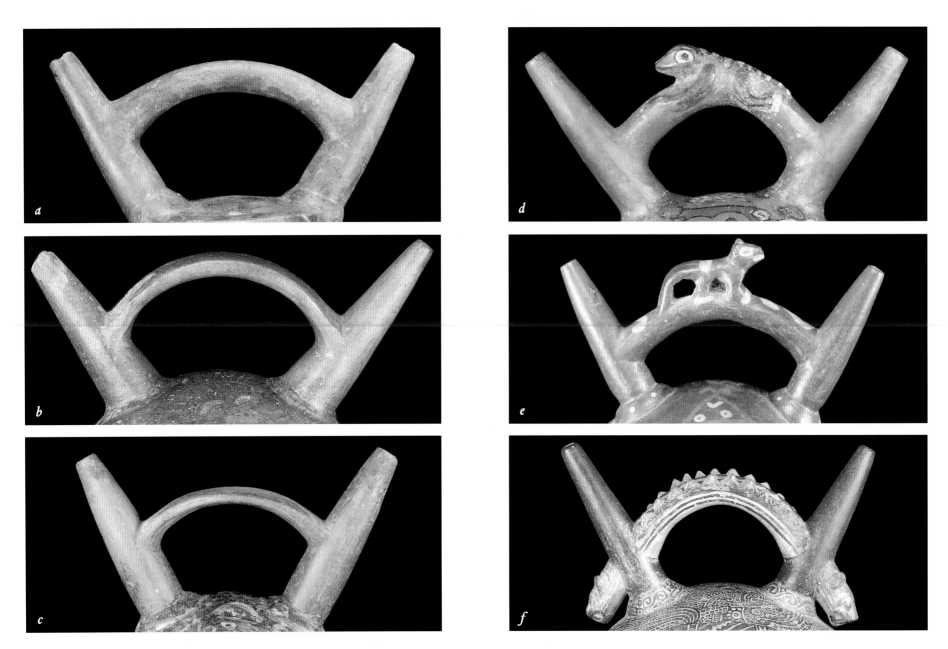

2.13   *Spouts of double spout and bridge bottles.*

The chambers of double spout and bridge bottles are topped by two conical spouts set at an angle and connected by a bridge-like handle. The bridge may have a round, rectangular, or flat cross-section [2.13a–c]. Sometimes modeled lizards or felines are on top of the bridge [2.13d–e]. On one example, the bridge is a double-headed serpent [2.13f] similar to the double-headed snake arch on a stirrup spout bottle [2.5h].

Other Huari-derived forms include cups [2.14a], pod-shaped vessels [2.14b], and a flask-shaped jar with a lug on its shoulder [2.14c].

2.14   *Huari-derived cup [a], pod-shaped vessel [b], and flask [c].*

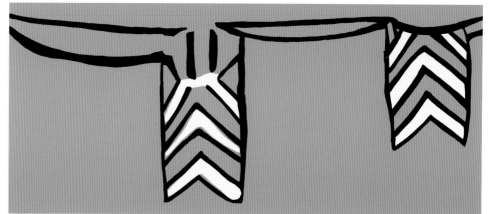

a Phase IV painting from Southern Moche Region.

b Phase V painting from Southern Moche Region.

c Late Moche painting from Moro.

MOCHE PAINTING STYLE

IN THE SOUTHERN MOCHE REGION, the realistic, open style of Phase IV fineline paintings [2.15a] continues into Phase V [2.15b]. In contrast, the figures depicted in many fineline paintings at Moro are densely packed [2.15c]. Moreover, they look like caricatures of similar figures painted in the Southern Moche Region. The background surrounding figures in Moro style paintings is often filled with abstract elements such as circles and dots, which tend to obscure the activity being depicted. These background filler elements, which seem to have no iconographic significance, have been omitted from most of the fineline drawings in this volume to enhance the clarity of the principal designs.

Fineline paintings on Moro vessels exhibit a wide range of quality. Some are so poor that the subject matter is difficult to recognize [2.16a].[5] Here, the artist rendered the design with uneven brush strokes that appear to be hastily applied; the smearing of slip in many areas further reduces clarity. The subject matter of some paintings is easy to identify, but the painter lacked artistic ability [2.16b]. Many talented artists, however, produced paintings of remarkable precision and clarity. For example, a particularly complex painting was rendered by its skillful artist on a smaller than average chamber [2.1a/2.15c].

2.15 Comparison of fineline painting styles.

2.16 *Crescent boat scenes by unskilled artists.*

2.17 *Paintings on angled chambers.*

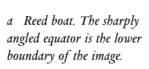

a   Reed boat. The sharply angled equator is the lower boundary of the image.

b   Crescent boat scene. The equator represents the crescent boat.

On vessels with round or curved chambers, the painting usually covers the entire surface; however, vessels with sharply angled equators are usually painted only on the upper half of the chamber. The sharp equator of the chamber often serves simply as the lower boundary of the image [2.17a]. This is the only reed boat scene we have found painted on a vessel with a sharply angled equator (see Reed Boats, p. 30); however, in several crescent boat scenes the curve of the sharply angled equator (as seen from above the level of the equator) actually represents the boat [2.17b] (see Crescent Boats, p. 44).

Most fineline paintings produced at Moro have two colors of slip: a red design on an off-white background [2.17b]. A few used the opposite: a white-on-red color scheme [2.18]. Some red-on-white vessels also have a third color, a light orange [2.19], similar to that used in some Phase IV paintings from the Southern Moche Region.[6]

2.18   Crescent boat painting with white design on red background.

2.19   Three-color crescent boat painting.

Although the ring bases of most Moro stirrup spout bottles were painted with solid red slip [2.20a], some were painted with fineline designs. About 10 percent were painted with waves [2.20b]. On some bottles with reed boat designs, the waves are partially on or just above the ring base [2.20c–d]. A few ring bases were painted with weapon bundles [2.20e],[7] bird heads [2.20f], or S-shaped elements [2.20g]. The chamber designs on several bottles in our sample continue down onto the ring bases

2.20 *Painted designs on ring bases.*

[2.20h–j and 3.8]. On the Burial Theme bottle in figure 2.20j (see The Burial Theme, p. 96), a coffin with ropes supporting it was painted on the ring base.

The bottoms of two vessels in our sample have painted designs [2.21a–b]. Both of these bottles have tubes through their chambers.

a   Bird warrior painted on bottom.

b   Flower motif painted on bottom.

2.21   Vessels with painted designs on bottom.

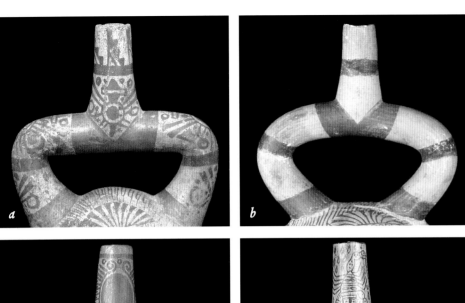

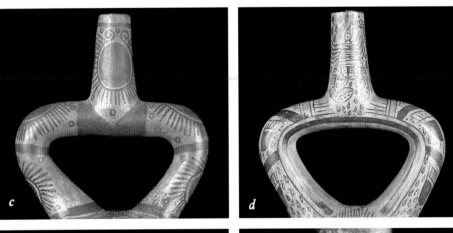

The paintings on Moro spouts are distinctive. More than 50 percent of the stirrup spouts are painted with weapon bundles and stripes [2.22a]. About 40 percent have stripes with no other motif [2.22b]. The few remaining vessels have a variety of motifs [e.g., 2.22c–h]. Most Moro stirrup spouts have spout designs with stripes encircling the arch and/or the upper spout. Exceptions are shown in figures 2.22d–e.[8]

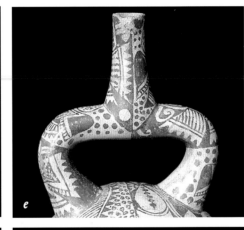

2.22 Painted designs on stirrup spouts.

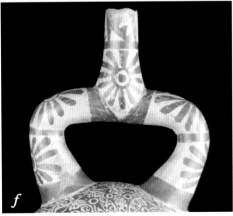

PAINTING STYLE DERIVED FROM HUARI

WITH THE APPEARANCE OF POLYCHROME HUARI CERAMICS on the north coast of Peru, Moche artists began painting vessels with polychrome slip [2.23].[9] Most Moro polychrome paintings are less detailed than two-color paintings.

The sequence in which colors were applied on polychrome vessels can be determined by examining the areas where colors overlap. Typically, the artist first painted the vessel with a background color and then applied the various colored slips to create the image. Finally, he outlined each color area with black slip.[10] The black slip usually hid the borders of the underlying colors. The fish design on the bottle in figure 2.24 is an example of this technique; however, the slip was too thin and the black outline did not fully obscure the borders of the colored areas.

2.23 *Jar with weapon bundle design painted in polychrome.*

2.24 *Moche stirrup spout vessel with polychrome painted design.*

3   Subject Matter

IN THE SOUTHERN MOCHE REGION, the first two phases of Moche fineline painting emphasized supernatural rather than human activities. The percentage of paintings depicting human activity then increased dramatically into Phase IV, when there were nearly as many paintings of human activities as there were of supernatural activities. This trend suddenly reversed at the end of Phase IV, and in Phase V nearly all fineline paintings once again depicted supernatural activities.[1] The fineline paintings at Moro also reflect this shift; nearly all depict supernatural activities.

In the Southern Moche Region, between Phases IV and V, there was also a dramatic increase in the frequency of paintings depicting marine activities. That increase is strongly reflected at Moro. About 64 percent of the paintings in our Moro sample relate to the ocean.

The inventory of activities depicted at Moro was reduced, compared with Phase IV paintings from the Southern Moche Region. Several important Phase IV activities were rarely portrayed at Moro or were represented by only a few residual elements (see Musical Processions, p. 93; Ritual Runners, p. 94; and The Warrior Narrative, p. 114). On the other hand, entirely new activities reached their fullest expression at Moro (see The Burial Theme, p. 96; and The Waved Spiral Narrative, p. 117).

The bulk of the subject matter in Moro fineline painting is Moche, but some is clearly derived from the Huari style and often results in interesting Moche-Huari combinations.

BOATS

DEPICTIONS OF BOATS COMPOSE the largest group of fineline paintings in our Moro sample.[2] These can be divided into two types: reed boats and crescent boats. They are superficially similar but are sufficiently distinct to be considered separately.

REED BOATS

Reed boats appeared in Moche fineline paintings in the Southern Moche Region as early as Phase III and continued through Phase V. They usually depicted fishing or scenes involving natural fish and birds.[3] Moro reed boat scenes, however, do not include those activities, with one exception [3.8]. Although reed boats were much more frequently depicted at Moro than they were in the Southern Moche Region, they exhibit less variation. Moro reed boat scenes usually feature two boats, one on each side of the chamber [2.4a, 2.17a, 3.1–2, 3.4–21, 4.13, 4.32]. A single elaborately dressed individual occupies each boat. All reed boats except a few that appear in the Waved Spiral Narrative (p. 117) have lower decks or cargo holds, which carry jars or other objects. Modeled heads inside the vessel in figure 2.4a suggest that some reed boats transported passengers.

Net-covered floats are attached to most of the reed boats. All of the boats have animal heads on the upturned bow and stern. In all but one example [3.2c], one end of the boat has two heads and the other end has one head. About half of the boats have human legs or arms. The boats in four paintings have both legs and arms [3.1, 3.7–8, 3.127]. Nine paintings depict boats with legs but no arms [3.4, 3.11, 3.15–21]. The boats in the Waved Spiral Narrative have arms but no legs [3.123–124, 4.25–26]. When present, arms are usually on both ends of the boat. Reed boats are usually separated by rays [e.g., 3.1].

A boatman we have called Paddler always occupies at least one of the boats. He kneels on a net deck[4] and propels the boat with a long animal-headed paddle. He is surrounded by clubs and shields or weapon bundles. Wave motifs frequently decorate the top of his headdress.

A seated female usually occupies the other boat. She sits rather than kneels and is often surrounded by radiating lines that are either plain [3.2a] or end in serpent heads [3.2b]. Weapon bundles surround her in one painting [3.2c]. She often wears a net dress and a unique plumed headdress with a tiered train hanging down her back [3.2a–c]. A snake sash may be under the tiered train [3.2b]. Sometimes she has dragonfly wings on her back and holds a goblet [3.2d].

Although many crescent boat scenes are painted on sharply angled chambers (see p. 44), our sample contains only a single reed boat scene on an angled chamber [2.17a]. All the others are on spherical chambers, oblate chambers, or chambers with curved equators.

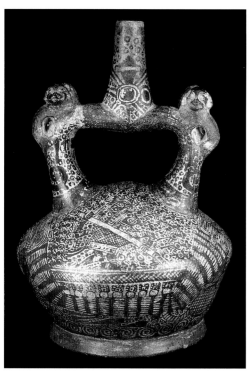

3.1 *Reed boat scene by the Rodriguez Painter (see p. 161). The boats have both arms and legs.*

a   Detail of figure 3.10.

b   Detail of figure 2.17a.

c   Detail of figure 3.12.

d   Detail of figure 3.15.

3.2   Reed boats carrying cargo. These paintings illustrate variations in the female occupant.

3.3 *Figures with textile-wrapped containers (not from Moro).*

a

b

In some paintings, the female has an object in front of her that appears to be an open bag [3.2b, d]. Although these bags are not clearly portrayed in the Moro paintings, they are the same textile-wrapped containers frequently depicted in Moche art from the Southern Moche Region [3.3]. Textile-wrapped containers are consistently shown in the lap or in front of a figure who is holding an object in his hand, possibly a sacrificial chisel or a spatula. In some representations [e.g., 3.3b], the figure seems to be using the object to transfer something from the container to his mouth.

3.4 *Reed boat scene.*

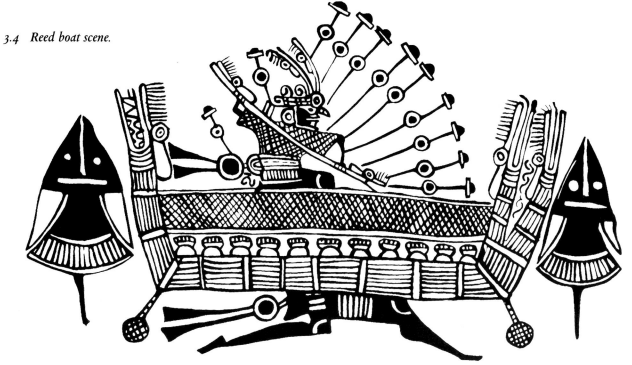

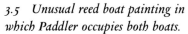

3.5 *Unusual reed boat painting in which Paddler occupies both boats.*

3.6 *Unusual reed boat painting in which Paddler occupies both boats. The other side of the chamber was too badly spalled to be drawn, but it was possible to identify Paddler as the occupant of the second boat.*

In most of the paintings in our sample, Paddler occupies one boat, and the female occupies the other. There are, however, two examples in which Paddler occupies both boats [3.5–6].[5]

In most reed boat paintings, no means of propulsion is indicated for the female's craft. Only one painting in our sample shows her with a paddle [3.7].[6] The legs appended to many reed boats may be intended to suggest forward motion.

3.7 Unusual reed boat painting in which both Paddler and the female figure paddle their boats. In this painting, Paddler's headdress lacks the usual wave motifs.

The reed boat shown in figure 3.8 is very different from the others in our sample. It is rendered in Huari-derived polychrome instead of bichrome. The upper spout is decorated with modeled figures and manioc tubers, and the spout arches are painted with plant motifs. The most dramatically different feature of the painting is the female. Instead of kneeling passively, she is standing and fishing with a hook and line, and she is surrounded by fish. This is the only known exception to the previously stated rule that Moro reed boats are not used for fishing.

The faces of Paddler and the female are very similar to the figures of Iguana and Wrinkle Face[7] in the De Vault bottle paintings (see p. 82), suggesting that this bottle is related to that group.

3.8 Polychrome reed boats.

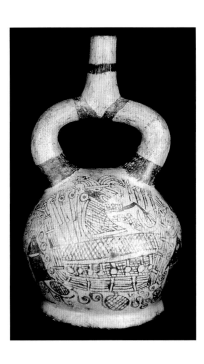

3.9 *Reed boat painting by an unskilled artist. The lines radiating from the female, the weapon bundles surrounding Paddler, and the rays between the boats are rendered inconsistently. Paddler's headdress lacks the wave motifs.*

3.10 *Reed boats. The cargos in the two boats are different, and Paddler's boat lacks net covered floats.*

3.11 Reed boats. Paddler and his boat are much smaller than the female and her boat.

3.12 Reed boats. Both Paddler and the female are surrounded by weapon bundles.

3.13   *Reed boat scene by the Large Lip Painter.*

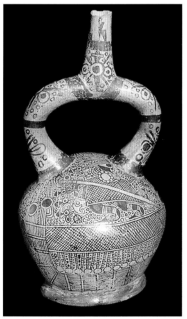

3.14   *Reed boat scene by the Large Lip Painter.*

3.15 Reed boat scene by the Reed Boat Painter.

3.16 Reed boat scene by the Reed Reed Boat Painter.

3.17   *Reed boat scene by the Reed Boat Painter.*

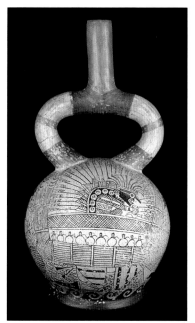

3.18   *Reed boat scene by the Reed Boat Painter.*

3.19　*Reed boat scene by the Reed Boat Painter.*

3.20　*Reed boat scene by the Reed Boat Painter. The spout is not Moro style and has probably been replaced.*

3.21 Sherds from a bottle with reed boats from a ceremonial plaza at El Brujo in La Huaca Cao Viejo in the Chicama Valley. The fineline painting is so similar to reed boats at Moro that the vessel was probably produced there. The sherds were found in a burial associated with late architecture.

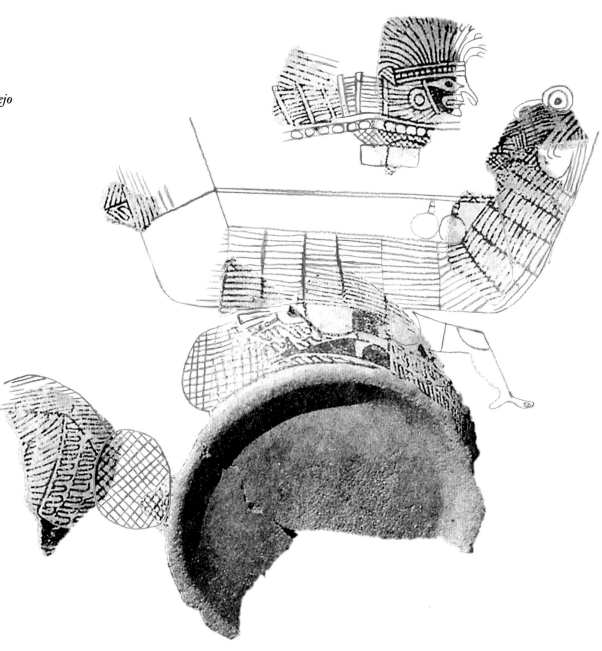

CRESCENT BOATS

Crescent boats compose about 71 percent of the boats depicted on ceramic vessels from Moro and about 25 percent of our total sample of Moro fineline paintings [2.2a, 2.2c, 2.16a–b, 2.17b, 2.18–19, 3.22–45, 3.47–48, 4.1–12, 4.14, 4.18–19, 4.27–31].[8] These boats appear only in Moro fineline painting; no known examples are from the Southern Moche Region. Crescent boats are not combined in paintings with reed boats.

Many crescent boats are painted on the upper surface of sharply angled chambers [3.22–25, 3.27]. The crescent-shaped boat may be painted explicitly [e.g., 3.22, 3.26] or the boat may by represented by the curvature of the angled equator as seen from above [e.g., 3.23]. A vessel excavated at Moro has a row of S-shaped wave symbols just below the equator [3.27]. Crescent boat scenes on chambers with curved equators [3.28–32] and on oblate [3.33] and spherical chambers [3.34–41] nearly always cover the whole chamber and explicitly depict the crescent. Our only exceptions are a boat scene on the upper half of a curved chamber [3.26] and a boat scene that does not explicitly depict the boat, even though the design extends well below the equator [3.28]. We have found only two crescent boat paintings that are not on stirrup spout bottles. One is on a flask-shaped jar with lugs on the shoulders [3.42], and the other is on a double spout and bridge bottle [3.43].

Paddler is not seen in crescent boats. Only the female occupies them, except for two paintings in which each boat contains a Crested Animal [3.44–45].

Although there is overall uniformity in the depictions of crescent boats, many details vary. In most paintings, the female wears a tightly woven net dress. In figure 3.29, however, one of the two females wears an open-net dress. In figure 3.35, the female's dress seems to be covered with disks, and the rays emanating from her and from the boat terminate in what appear to be bird heads. In most crescent boat scenes, however, the rays or lines emanating from the female and the boat are either plain [3.22] or terminate in serpent heads [3.37]. These serpent heads are often highly abstract [3.28]. The female sometimes has a rectangular object on her net dress and/or an open "bag" in front of her [3.47a], features that are also present in some reed boat paintings (see p. 33). Generally, the depiction of the female is very similar in reed boat and crescent boat scenes.

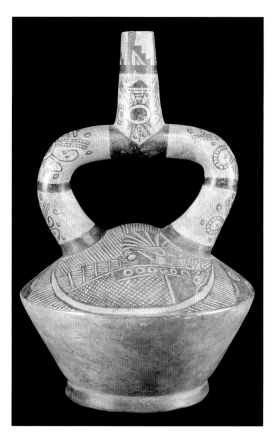

3.22 *Crescent boats on a vessel with a sharply angled chamber. The boats are painted explicitly.*

3.23 *Crescent boats. The boats are represented by the curvature of the vessel's sharply angled equator.*

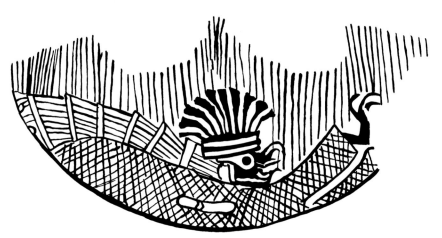

3.24 *Crescent boat scene by the Rodriguez Painter.*
The boats are represented by the sharply angled equator.

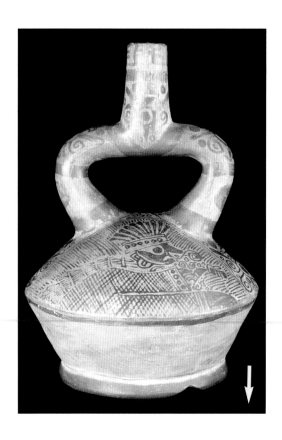

In the unique painting in figure 3.26, the female wears a headdress with wave motifs identical to the headdress worn by Paddler in reed boat scenes. In all other examples in Moro art, the female wears a headdress with an array of square tipped plumes.

3.25 Crescent boats. The boats are represented by the curvature of the sharply angled equator.

3.26 Crescent boats on the upper half of a chamber with a curved equator. The boats are painted explicitly.

3.27 *Crescent boats. The boats are represented by the curvature of the angled equator. S-shaped motifs beneath the boats may represent water.*

3.28 *Crescent boats. The boats are not depicted explicitly even though the painting extends below the equator.*

3.29 *Crescent boats on a softly angled chamber.*
One of the females wears an unusual open net shirt.

3.30 *Crescent boat scene by the Rodriguez Painter.*

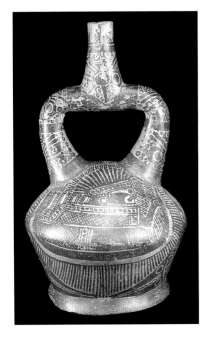

3.31 Crescent boat painting on a chamber with a curved equator. The spout has been replaced or repainted.

3.32 Crescent boats on a chamber with a curved equator.

3.33   *Crescent boats on an oblate chamber.*

3.34   *Crescent boats on a spherical chamber.*

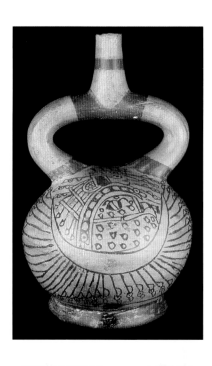

3.35 *Crescent boats on a spherical chamber.*

3.36 *Crescent boats on a spherical chamber. The spout is probably restored.*

3.37   *Crescent boat scene by the Reed Boat Painter.*

3.38   *Crescent boat scene by the Reed Boat Painter.*

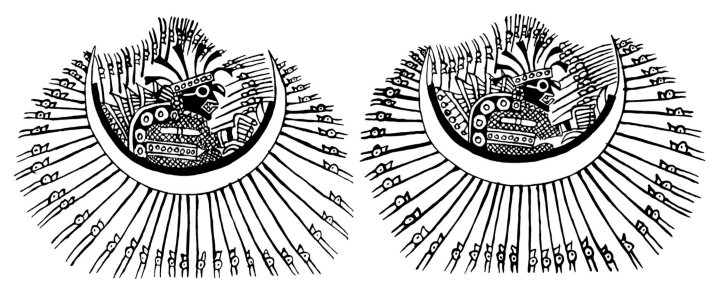

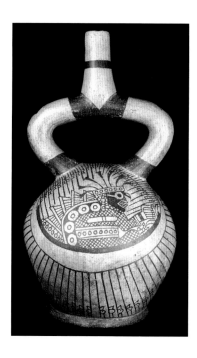

3.39 *Crescent boat scene by the Reed Boat Painter.*

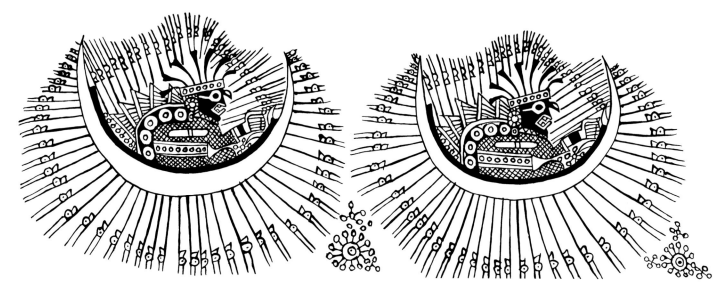

3.40 *Crescent boats on a spherical chamber.*

3.41 Crescent boat scene reconstructed from the sherds of a spherical stirrup spout vessel.

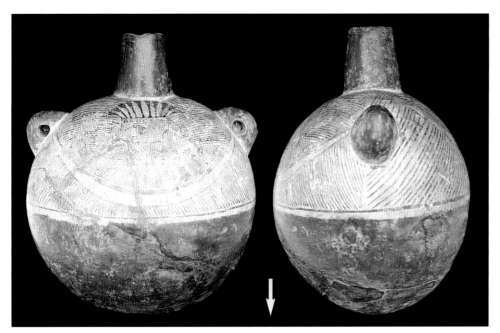

3.42 *Crescent boats on flask-shaped vessel.*

3.43 *Crescent boats on double spout and bridge vessel.*

Two paintings from Moro depict Crested Animals [3.44–45]. Moro Crested Animals are different from those from the Southern Moche Region [3.46] but have clearly evolved from them.[9] The Moro on the vessels are not easy to see because of the dense compositions and the presence of enigmatic objects.

The two figures above the Crested Animals in figure 3.45 resemble birds, but they lack wings. No similar objects are shown in representations of the Crested Animal from the Southern Moche Region. The identifiers of the Crested Animal in the two Moro paintings are the angled appendages emanating from the head and tail of the feline body. These appendages identified the Crested Animal in earlier phases, as well, where it was often portrayed in a crescent (moon?) [3.46]. In the Moro examples, the crescent is a crescent boat in the presence of ocean symbols.

3.44   Crested Animals in crescent boats.

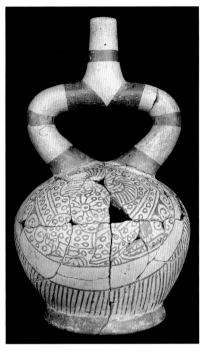

3.45 *Crested Animals in crescent boats.*

3.46 *Phase IV painting from the Southern Moche Region of Crested Animals in moonlike crescents.*

Unlike reed boats, crescent boats do not have arms, legs, heads, floats, net decks, or cargo holds; however, in some paintings the boats are separated by circular objects (gourds?) supported by ropes [3.47a], similar to those carried in the holds of reed boats. Crescent boats may be separated by other objects, such as spiders [3.47b], weapon bundles [3.47c], sea anemones [3.47d], rays [3.47e], or composites of sea anemones and rays [3.47f].

Both reed boats and crescent boats are shown moving from left to right, with a few exceptions [2.19, 3.48a–b, 3.123].

a Gourds suspended by ropes (detail of figure 4.1).

b Spiders (detail of figure 3.27).

c Weapon bundles (detail of figure 3.25).

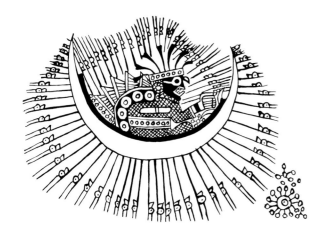

d Sea anemones (detail of figure 3.39).

e Rays (detail of figure 3.36).

f Ray and sea anemone composites (detail of figure 3.29).

3.47 *Objects used to separate crescent boats.*

3.48 *Crescent boat paintings in which the direction of motion is from right to left.*

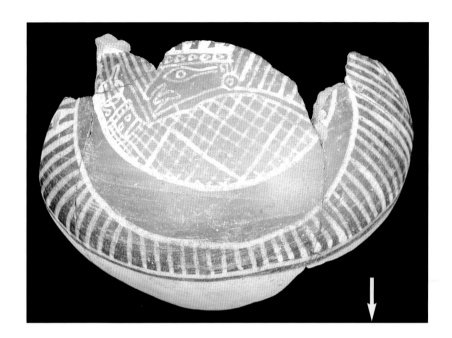

a Crescent boat painting on sharply angled chamber.

b Sherd painted with white-on-red crescent boat design.

SUPERNATURAL CONFRONTATION

SUPERNATURAL CONFRONTATION IS AN IMPORTANT marine activity in Moro fineline paintings. It involves two pairs of supernatural creatures fighting each other with tumis [2.2b, 3.49–71, 3.127, 4.15–17, 4.24, 4.33–34]. The tumi, a knife with a curved blade, is used as a weapon only by supernatural figures. Wrinkle Face is always one of the combatants, usually in both pairs; however, in two paintings, Wrinkle Face fights in one pair and Iguana in the other [3.52, 3.59]. Wrinkle Face and Iguana may represent terrestrial creatures.[10] Their opponents, however, are consistently marine creatures. In order of their frequency of occurrence, these marine creatures are:

- *Circular Creature*: an anthropomorphized animal that may represent a variety of gastropods such as snails or limpets [3.49–56, 3.69, 4.33–34]. The striped objects protruding behind the Circular Creature may represent the soft tissue of a gastropod.

- *Anthropomorphized Wave*: a new marine creature seen for the first time in Moro paintings [3.56–62, 3.69, 3.127, 4.15–17, 4.24]. Its most distinctive feature is a long band with fish inside. Small waves often border each side of the band. This band extends from the crotch [3.59] or waist [3.57a] of a humanlike body, or the band encloses the body from the waist down [3.57b]. In some paintings, only a head is attached directly to the band [3.57c]. In one example, the concept has been abbreviated to the point that the band is headless [3.57d].[11] One sherd from Moro that clearly shows this creature's head [3.58a] can be identified by comparing it with a similar intact painting [3.58b] (see Anthropomorphized Wave Painter, p. 170). The arching position of some Anthropomorphized Waves evokes an image of a strong crashing wave.

- *Strombus Monster*: a creature with a *Strombus* shell on its back [3.61–64, 3.71, 4.15].

- *Paddler*: a humanlike creature who fights with his fish-shaped paddle [2.2b, 3.51, 3.53–54, 3.65–67] (see Reed Boats, p. 30). He is always surrounded by weapon bundles.

- *Anthropomorphized Crab*: a creature who fights with its claws [3.52, 3.60, 3.65–67].

- *Sea Urchin*: an anthropomorphized humanlike creature whose body is surrounded by spines [3.55, 3.68, 3.70, 4.24].

The two creatures fighting Wrinkle Face or Iguana in each painting may be the same, such as Circular Creature [3.49–50], or different, such as Circular Creature and Paddler [3.51].

Background elements in Supernatural Confrontation scenes include ocean symbols, such as sea anemones [3.49, 3.53, 3.55, 3.57–60, 3.66–68], S-shaped wave symbols [3.50, 3.52–53, 3.55–56, 3.64, 3.67–68, 4.33], and *Strombus* shells [3.60, 3.68, 4.24], as well as symbols not related to the ocean, such as dogs [3.51, 3.54, 3.61, 3.66, 3.69], weapon bundles [3.51, 3.53–54, 3.65–67], sand symbols [3.65–66], and ulluchus [3.66] (see Plants, p. 146).

3.49 *Supernatural Confrontation: Wrinkle Face vs Circular Creature. A marine setting is suggested by sea anemones.*

3.50 *Supernatural Confrontation: Wrinkle Face vs Circular Creature. A marine setting is suggested by S-shaped wave motifs.*

Wrinkle Face's headdress usually consists of a headband, a feline head, and a fan-shaped element with streamers. Whenever Wrinkle Face is in conflict with Paddler, part of his headdress is missing [3.51, 3.53–54, 3.67] or his headdress has been knocked off [3.65–66].

3.51 Supernatural Confrontation: Wrinkle Face vs Circular Creature and Paddler.

In some confrontations with Anthropomorphized Crab [3.52], Anthropomorphized Wave [3.56], Circular Creature [3.56], or Strombus Monster [3.64], Wrinkle Face's headdress resembles a bicorn ("commodore's") hat with wave motifs. The fan-shaped element on the headdress may be a modification of the fan at the back of Wrinkle Face's regular headdress.

3.52 Supernatural Confrontation: Iguana vs Circular Creature and Wrinkle Face vs Anthropomorphized Crab.

3.53 *Supernatural Confrontation: Wrinkle Face vs Circular Creature and Paddler.*

3.54 *Supernatural Confrontation: Wrinkle Face vs Circular Creature and Paddler.*

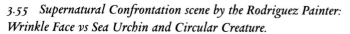

3.55 *Supernatural Confrontation scene by the Rodriguez Painter: Wrinkle Face vs Sea Urchin and Circular Creature.*

3.56 *Supernatural Confrontation: Wrinkle Face vs Anthropomorphized Wave and Circular Creature.*

a   Detail of figure 3.60.

b   Detail of figure 3.56.

c   Detail of figure 3.61.

d   Detail of figure 3.62.

3.57   Variations in Anthropomorphized Wave depictions in Supernatural Confrontation

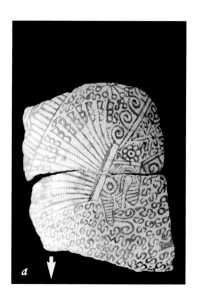

3.58   *Identification of Anthropomorphized Wave sherd.*

3.59 *Supernatural Confrontation by the Amano Painter: Anthropomorphized Wave vs Iguana and Wrinkle Face.*

3.60 *Supernatural Confrontation: Wrinkle Face vs Anthropomorphized Wave and Anthropomorphized Crab.*

3.61 *Supernatural Confrontation: Wrinkle Face vs Anthropomorphized Wave and Strombus Monster.*

3.62 *Supernatural Confrontation: Wrinkle Face vs Anthropomorphized Wave and Strombus Monster.*

3.63 *Supernatural Confrontation: Wrinkle Face vs Strombus Monster.*

3.64 *Supernatural Confrontation: Wrinkle Face vs Strombus Monster.*

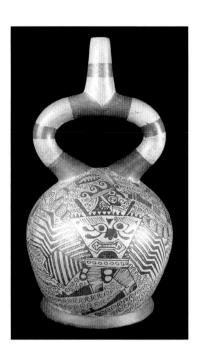

3.65 *Supernatural Confrontation: Paddler and Anthropomorphized Crab vs Wrinkle Face.*

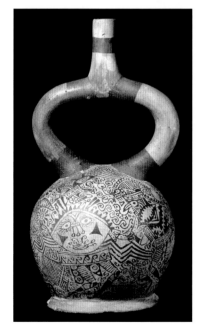

3.66 *Supernatural Confrontation: Paddler and Anthropomorphized Crab vs Wrinkle Face.*

3.67 *Supernatural Confrontation scene by the Moro Painter:*
Paddler and Anthropomorphized Crab vs Wrinkle Face.

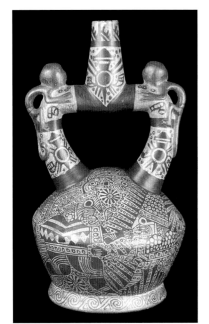

3.68 *Supernatural Confrontation scene by the*
Burial Theme Painter: Wrinkle Face vs Sea Urchin.

3.69 *Supernatural Confrontation scene on a double spout and bridge vessel: Iguana vs Circular Creature and Anthropomorphized Wave vs Wrinkle Face.*

3.70 *Supernatural Confrontation: Wrinkle Face vs Sea Urchin.*

3.71 *Supernatural Confrontation: Wrinkle Face vs Strombus Monster.*

BEAN AND STICK CEREMONY

THE BEAN AND STICK CEREMONY involves pairs of figures who hold short sticks and either hold or are surrounded by beans. In the Southern Moche Region, this ceremony is present in Phase IV fineline paintings, but it doesn't seem to continue into Phase V. Phase IV paintings may involve Wrinkle Face and a variety of other supernatural and anthropomorphized creatures.[12] It is a significant activity in Moro paintings, but only Wrinkle Face and Iguana participate. The Bean and Stick Ceremony was rendered in both bichrome and polychrome slip painting at Moro.

BICHROME PAINTINGS

In most Moro bichrome fineline paintings of the Bean and Stick Ceremony, both Wrinkle Face and Iguana participate [3.72–75, 3.77, 3.79, 4.21–22]. In two paintings, both figures are Wrinkle Face [3.76, 3.78]. The participants always hold two sticks in each hand, and both hands are always shown. Beans fill the background. Most of the figures are on top of stepped daises, which are painted with various designs [e.g., 3.72].[13] The ceremony was painted with two-color slip on both stirrup spout bottles and double spout and bridge bottles [e.g., 3.73].

The participants may lie across the daises or they may be seated on the daises [3.74–75]. Moro artists introduced a new seated position in this ceremony, showing a frontal view of the figure's torso and arms, combined with a top view of his folded legs [3.74–75, 3.77]. The position is also evident in the figure under the roofed structure in a Burial Theme scene [3.112].

Most Phase IV depictions of the Bean and Stick Ceremony involve two pairs of figures, with the members of each pair facing each other. Most Moro depictions show only two individuals, who are both facing to the right and thus not facing each other [3.72–74, 3.76, 3.78–79, 4.21–22]. In one painting, however, Wrinkle Face and Iguana sit facing each other on each side of the bottle [3.75]. Another painting shows Wrinkle Face lying across both daises, with small Iguanas sitting in front of and below him in the folded-leg position [3.77].

3.72   *Bichrome Bean and Stick Ceremony by the Amano Painter:*
Wrinkle Face and Iguana in prone position on daises.

3.73   *Bichrome Bean and Stick Ceremony on a double spout and bridge bottle:*
Wrinkle Face and Iguana in prone position on daises.

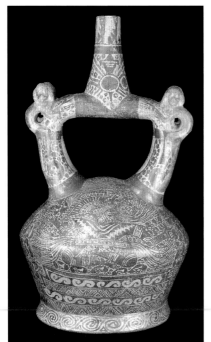

3.74 *Bichrome Bean and Stick Ceremony by the Rodriguez Painter:*
Iguana and Wrinkle Face in the folded-leg seated position.

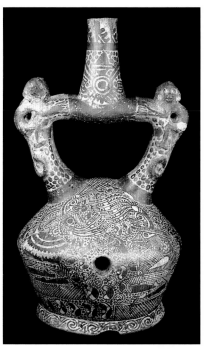

*3.75 Bichrome Bean and Stick Ceremony: Wrinkle Face and
Iguana in the folded-leg seated position facing each other.*

3.76 *Bichrome Bean and Stick Ceremony:*
Wrinkle Face prone on daises.

3.77 *Bichrome Bean and Stick Ceremony by the Rodriguez Painter:*
Wrinkle Face prone on daises, with Iguana in the folded-leg seated position.

In these two paintings [3.78–79], each figure is lying prone, presumably on a dais. The dais is not shown, however, but is represented by the equator of the vessel. Consequently, the design is only on the upper half of each chamber. These paintings are analogous to crescent boat paintings in which the equator of the vessel represents the boat [e.g., 3.23].

3.78 *Bichrome Bean and Stick Ceremony on a stirrup spout vessel with a sharply angled equator.*

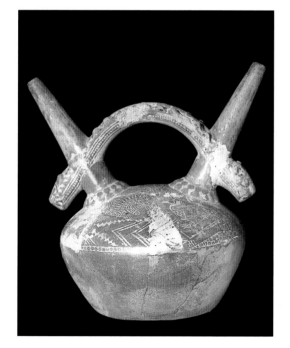

3.79 *Bichrome Bean and Stick Ceremony on a double spout and bridge bottle with a rounded equator: Wrinkle Face and Iguana in a prone position.*

Polychrome Paintings and the De Vault Bottle Group

There is another distinct group of ceramic vessels with the Bean and Stick Ceremony, which we call the De Vault Bottle Group.[14] They are all double spout and bridge bottles with ovoid chambers and are painted with polychrome slip [3.80–90].[15] The scene is the same on most of the vessels. Unlike the Moro bichrome paintings of the Bean and Stick Ceremony, the positions of Wrinkle Face and Iguana do not vary; they lie prone on top of daises holding sticks. Each figure holds four sticks, but only one hand is shown. It is not clear whether each hand holds fours sticks or whether the four sticks represent the total for both hands. Wrinkle Face and Iguana usually face each other. Beans surround them, and beans decorate the tops of most of the bridges between the spouts. The faces of the two figures are different from those in the bichrome Moro paintings, and the face of each is the same on every vessel. Wrinkle Face is not wrinkled, his nose is pendant, and his chin juts out. Iguana's lips are thin and pointed. Each has long lips that widen back into a triangular-shaped mouth with teeth. Several of these vessels are so similar that they may have been produced in the same workshop.

The variations from this basic description are minor. The cross-sections of the bridges may be flat [3.80–81], round [3.82], or rectangular [3.83]. Two vessels have frogs sitting on their bridges [3.82, 3.84]. In figure 3.85, Wrinkle Face and Iguana follow rather than face each other. The daises can have three, four, or five tiers [3.80–81, 3.86]. Only two vessels have decorated daises [3.85, 3.88]. The latter vessel is so ornate that it doesn't seem to belong to this group, but the faces of Wrinkle Face and Iguana are like all the others.

The same identifying faces can be found in other activities. A polychrome bottle similar to the De Vault Bean and Stick bottles displays two standing figures holding snake-headed arches festooned with manioc tubers [3.163]. Paddler and the female in the polychrome reed boat painting [3.8] may be related to this group. Paddler's face closely resembles that of Iguana, and the female's face closely resembles that of Wrinkle Face in the polychrome Bean and Stick Ceremony.

3.80 *Polychrome Bean and Stick Ceremony with a flat bridge and three-step daises.*

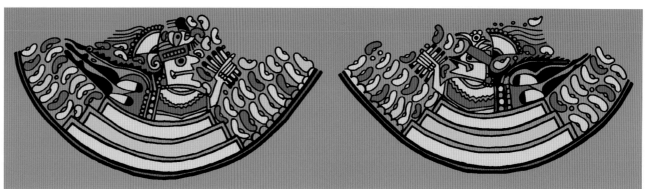

3.81 *Polychrome Bean and Stick Ceremony with a flat bridge and four-step daises.*

3.82 *Polychrome Bean and Stick Ceremony with round bridge.*

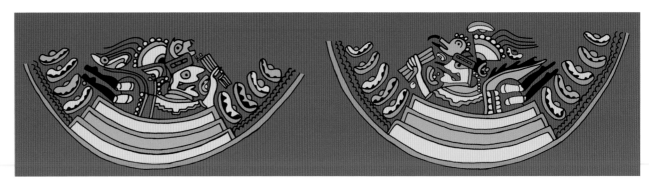

3.83 *Polychrome Bean and Stick Ceremony with rectangular bridge.*

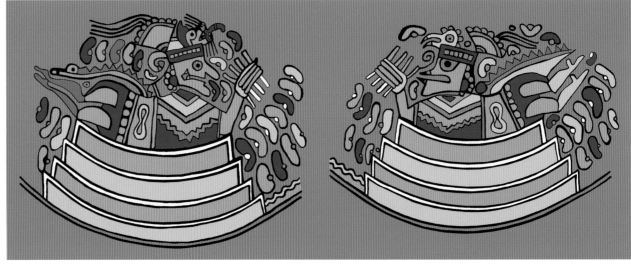

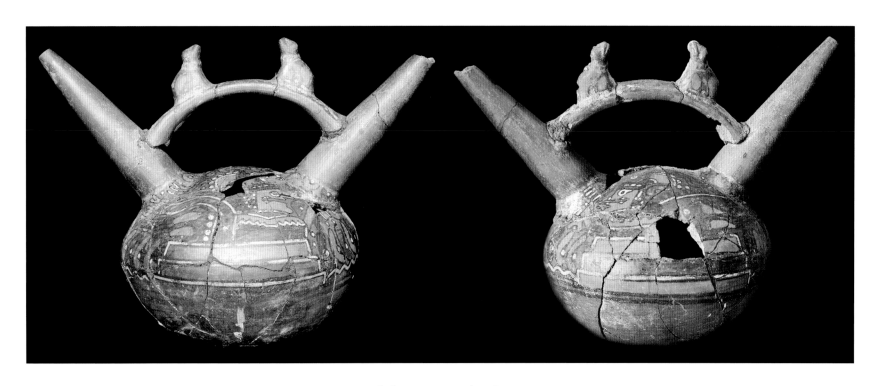

3.84 *Polychrome Bean and Stick Ceremony.*

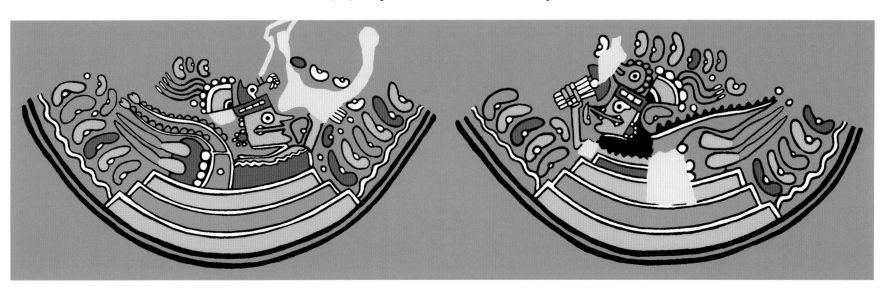

3.85 *Polychrome Bean and Stick Ceremony with decorated daises.*

3.86 *Polychrome Bean and Stick Ceremony with five-step daises.*

3.87 *Polychrome Bean and Stick Ceremony with flat bridge.*

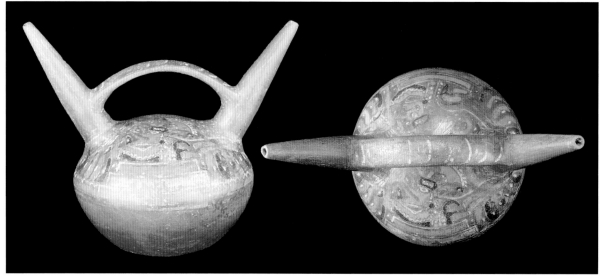

3.88 Ornate polychrome Bean and Stick Ceremony.

3.89 Polychrome Bean and Stick Ceremony.

3.90 Polychrome Bean and Stick Ceremony vessel excavated in the Rimac Valley.

CEREMONIAL BADMINTON

CEREMONIAL BADMINTON FEATURES ONE OR TWO major figures standing on daises holding spears and an atlatl (spear thrower) [3.91–92, 3.94–96].[16] Smaller figures follow or surround them ready to launch spears. Some of the spears are wrapped with a cord attached to a flowerlike object. The same type of object may appear in the background, suggesting that the launching of spears with these "flowers" is an important part of this ceremony. Sometimes the spears are blunt-ended and have crossbars [3.92].[17]

One Moro jar features three large "flowers" that resemble those in the badminton scene [3.93]. Objects similar or identical to these are also found in ocean scenes such as Supernatural Confrontation [e.g., 3.60, 3.68], where they are thought to represent sea anemones. The significance of sea anemones in Ceremonial Badminton, particularly when tied by long cords to spearlike objects, is perplexing;[18] however, some Ceremonial Badminton scenes contain other ocean symbols as well. In one scene [3.91], the daises enclose gourds or jars suspended by ropes, similar to those contained in the holds of reed boats [3.1] and used as separators between some crescent boats [3.47a]. Other badminton scenes contain shells [3.92] or S-shaped motifs [3.94], which are ocean or wave symbols in other types of scenes.

3.91 *Ceremonial Badminton scene by the Moro Painter: Wrinkle Face and Iguana standing on daises.*

3.92 *Wrinkle Face in Ceremonial Badminton scene.*

3.93 *Moro jar depicting flowerlike objects, possibly sea anemones.*

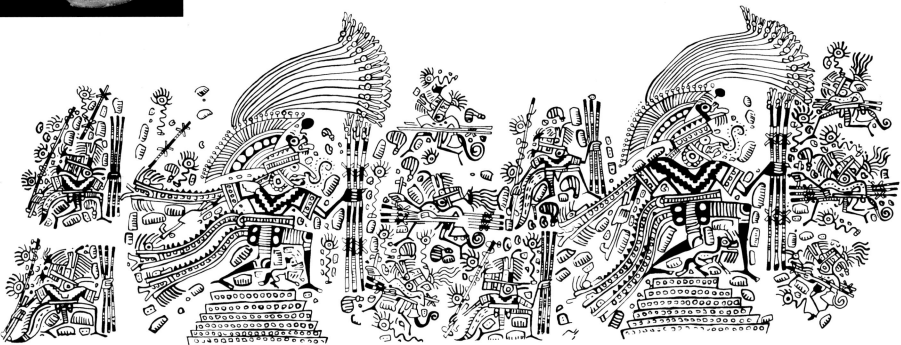

3.94 *Ceremonial Badminton scene showing S-shaped ocean symbols in the background.*

3.95 *Sherd found in fill at Moro illustrating a portion of Ceremonial Badminton.*

3.96 *Iguana and Wrinkle Face in Ceremonial Badminton scene. In this painting, only Wrinkle Face stands on a dais. The spout is partially restored.*

MUSICAL PROCESSIONS

IN PHASE IV PAINTINGS FROM THE Southern Moche Region, musicians were often depicted. Our Moro sample includes only one painting of a musical group. It shows Iguana and Wrinkle Face playing panpipes and anthropomorphized birds beating drums [3.97]. S-shaped wave motifs are in the background, again suggesting a possible ocean relationship.

3.97   Iguana and Wrinkle Face in a musical procession.

THE MOST COMMON FINELINE ACTIVITY in Phase IV paintings from the Southern Moche Region involves rows or spirals of either human runners or anthropomorphized animal runners carrying objects [3.98]. The human and animal runners wear distinctive headdresses often composed of a head ring supporting a large trapezoidal or circular element. Some runners wear wrapped headdresses, but all the headdresses are tied under the chin. Long ribbons stream down the back and cinch in at the waist. The ends of the ribbons float freely above the hips. The runners are almost always shirtless.

3.98   Typical Phase IV ritual runners from the Southern Moche Region.

In the Moro sample, there is only one vessel showing Ritual Runners [3.99].[9] The runners are humans, but they do not wear the "runner's uniform." Their headdresses are different, without the ribbons down the back, and the runners seem to wear shirts. The large trapezoidal element has been reduced to a small, white trapezoid on the side of each headdress. Two runners wear triangular objects attached to their belts. The objects attached to the other two belts may be ribbons. With one arm extended in front holding a bag, it is clear that these runners are a Moro painter's interpretation of the individuals in the running activity. Ulluchus surround the runners (see Plants, p. 146).

3.99   Moro depiction of ritual runners.

NARRATIVE SCENES

ARTISTS IN THE SOUTHERN MOCHE REGION developed the idea of depicting a narrative that occurred over a span of time rather than at a single moment. An important example, the Warrior Narrative, may have begun as early as Phase I–II[20] and continued through Phase IV.[21] In most cases, the parts of the narrative were expressed in a series of separate paintings. A unique Phase IV vessel depicts essentially the entire Warrior Narrative in one painting.[22]

Only residual elements of the Warrior Narrative remained at Moro (see p. 114); however, Moro artists used the narrative concept in two new types of scenes: the Burial Theme and the Waved Spiral Narrative (p. 117). In these paintings, the narrative consists of a group of individual events that are depicted on one vessel. We can identify these paintings as narratives because the same participants appear in more than one of the individual events, implying that time is passing between each event [3.100].

Although several elements of these two scenes occurred in earlier phases in the Southern Moche Region, it was only in the final phase that Moro artists (and, in one example [3.104], an artist in the Southern Moche Region) combined these elements to make a single narrative.

THE BURIAL THEME

One of the most complex scenes painted by Moro artists is that referred to as the Burial Theme. We published a detailed analysis of this scene in 1979, based on seven examples that were known at that time.[23] Since then, nine more examples have been identified, bringing the total to sixteen [3.101–117], including a sherd that illustrates a portion of the Burial Theme [3.106].

All of the artists who illustrated this complex burial ceremony adhered to a new kind of layout.[24] Double lines resembling those that separate the panels of a cartoon strip divide the ceremony into four parts [3.100]. On one side of the chamber are two activities, which we have called Burial and Assembly. The Burial activity depicts two figures (usually Wrinkle Face and Iguana) lowering a body or coffin into a tomb. They may hold an animal, probably a llama, on a rope behind them.[25] Assembly shows the funeral party flanking the tomb. The remaining two parts of the scene, Conch Shell Transfer and Sacrifice, are on the opposite side of the chamber. An elite figure engaging in the transfer of conch shells is seated on top of a stepped dais. In the section above him a naked female with splayed legs is being pecked by vultures, while Iguana or an anthropomorphized weapon leads a roped procession of vultures.[26] Wrinkle Face, Iguana, or both appear in at least three and usually all four activities on each bottle, suggesting that the painting is narrating a sequence of events.

3.100   *Layout of Burial Theme paintings.*

Fourteen of the sixteen known Burial Theme bottles appear to have come from Moro, including two that were excavated archaeologically. The vessel illustrated in figure 3.101 was found in a niche in the tomb of an elite female. It had been deliberately placed upside down, standing on its spout [3.102]. The other came from a cache not associated with a burial [3.103].

3.101 Burial Theme bottle excavated from the tomb of an elite female at Moro.

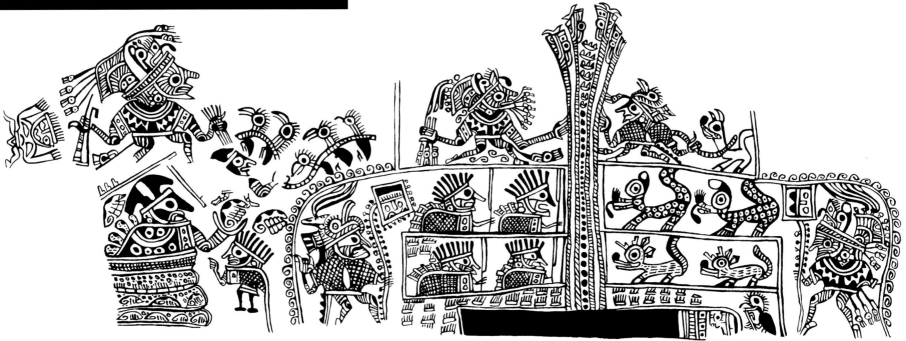

Burial Theme bottle placed in niche in inverted position.

3.102 Tomb of an elite female. The Burial Theme bottle in figure 3.101 is shown in its original inverted position in a niche at the head end of the tomb.

Iguana leads the vulture processions in the Sacrifice sections of figures 3.103 and 3.114. S-shaped wave motifs appear in the backgrounds of figures 3.103, 3.111–112, and 3.116–117.

3.103 *Burial Theme bottle excavated from a cache at Moro.*

In our original study of the Burial Theme, we thought that one bottle strongly resembled Phase IV paintings, so we assumed that it was the earliest Burial Theme painting [3.104]. Now, because of the form of the bottle, the placement of the stirrup, the spout decoration, and the painting style, it seems more likely that it is from the Southern Moche Region and not from Moro.

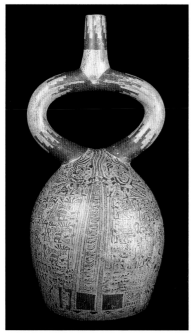

3.104   Stirrup spout bottle from the Southern Moche Region illustrating the Burial Theme.

3.105 *Burial Theme bottle.*

3.106 *Burial Theme sherd from Huaca Facho in the Lambayeque Valley.*

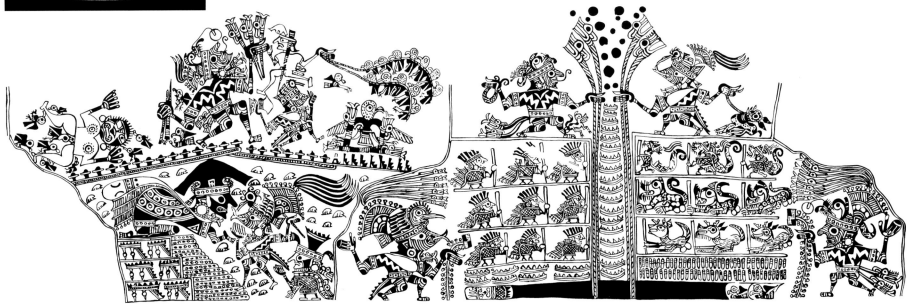

In addition to the fifteen Burial Theme bottles, a sherd illustrating the sacrificed female from a Burial Theme bottle has been reported from the site of Huaca Facho in the Lambayeque Valley about eighty kilometers north of Moro [3.106].[27] That bottle may have come originally from Moro.

3.107 Burial Theme bottle with a painted design on the bottom and a tube through the chamber.

3.108 *Burial Theme bottle.*
The spout has been replaced.

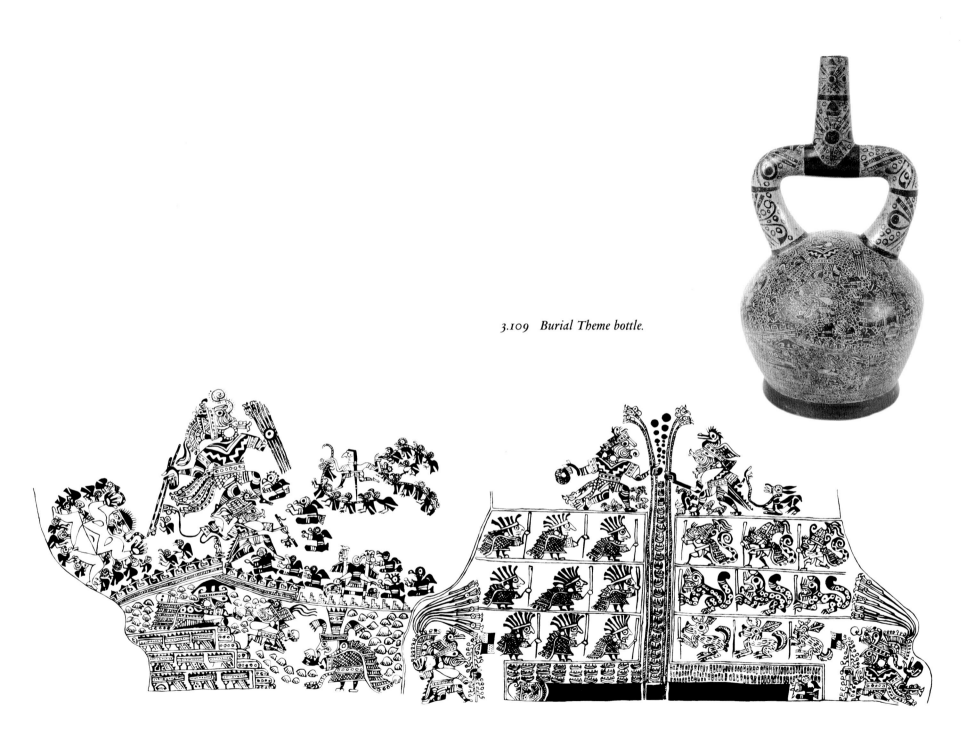

3.109   *Burial Theme bottle.*

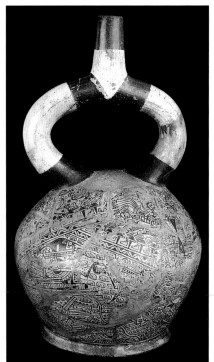

3.110 *Burial Theme bottle.*
The spout has been replaced.

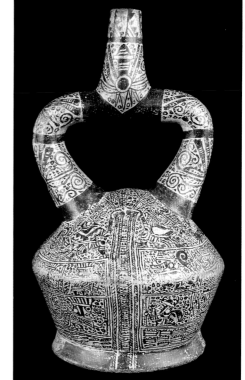

3.111 *Burial Theme bottle.*

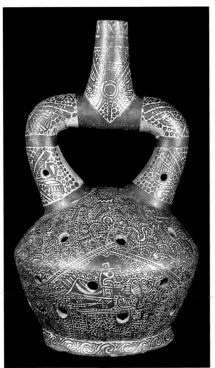

3.112 *Burial Theme bottle with a chamber inside the outer chamber and a spout inside the outer spout. Forty-two small holes perforate the outer chamber and outer spout.*

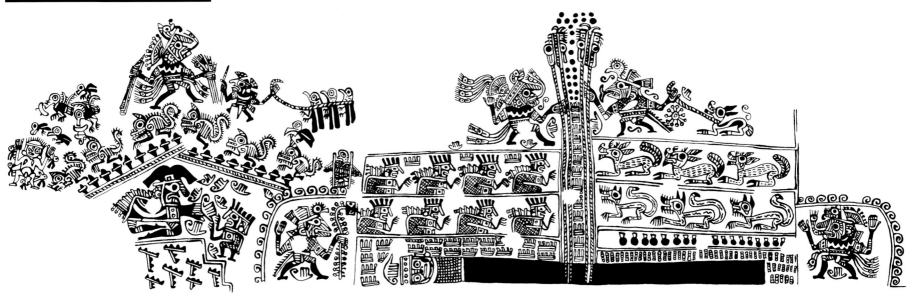

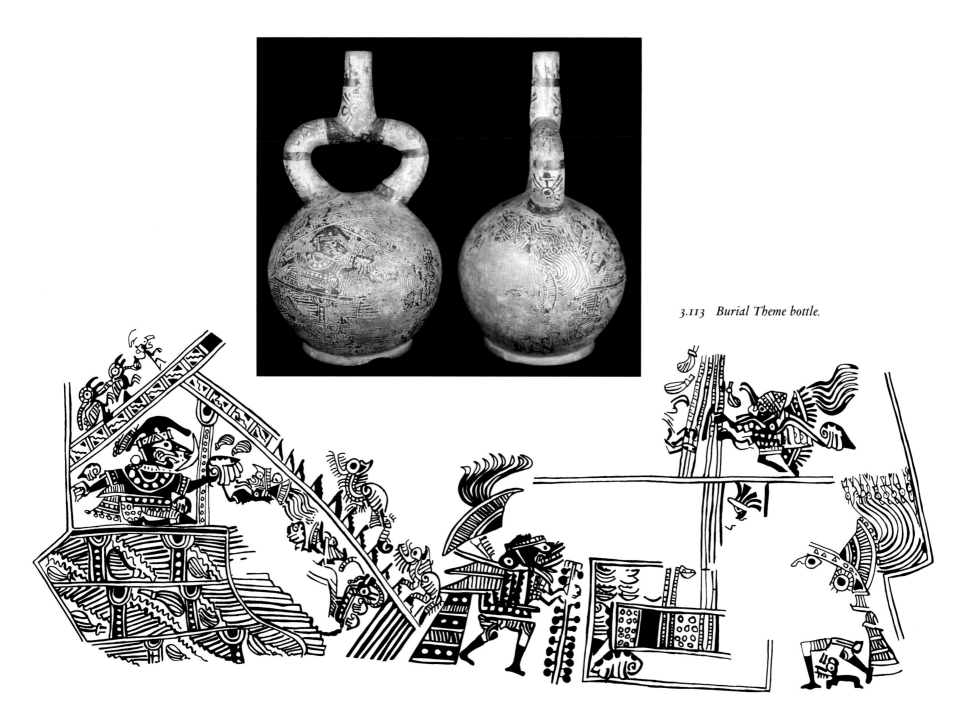

3.113 *Burial Theme bottle.*

3.114 Burial Theme bottle.

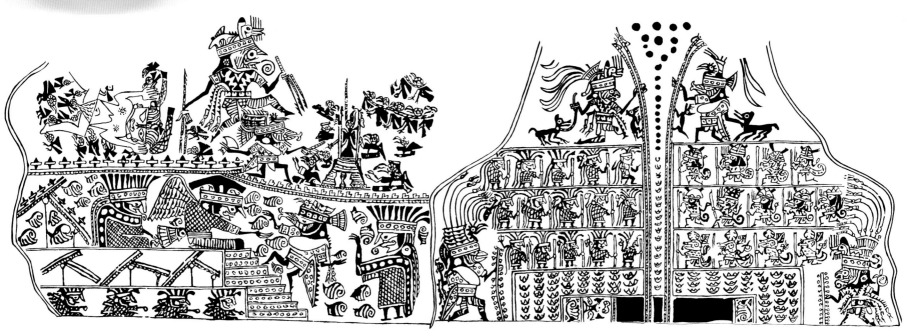

3.115 *Burial Theme bottle.*
The spout has been replaced.

3.116 *Burial Theme bottle by the Burial Theme Painter.*

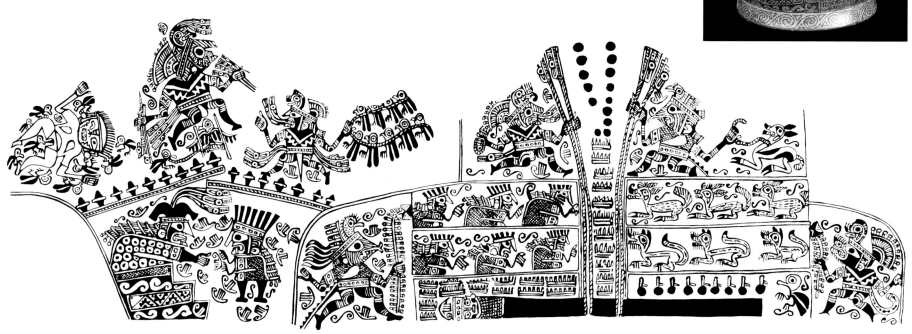

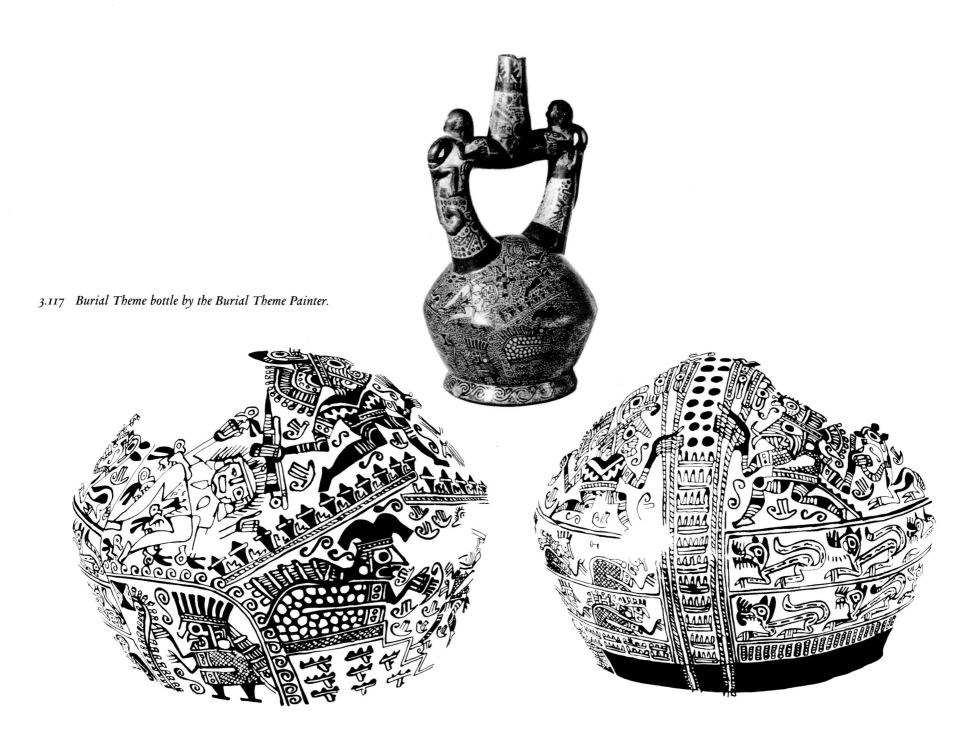

3.117 *Burial Theme bottle by the Burial Theme Painter.*

THE WARRIOR NARRATIVE

The depiction of warriors and combat began early in Moche art and proliferated greatly in Phase IV.[28] Many vessels depicted one or more parts of the Warrior Narrative: warriors preparing for battle, fighting, parading and sacrificing captives, and offering the captives' blood in goblets to important personages in the Sacrifice Ceremony. The final event of the Warrior Narrative is the dismemberment of sacrificial victims.

Our Moro sample contains only one painting illustrating warriors and combat [3.118]. Otherwise, only a few residual elements of the Warrior Narrative were depicted, but some of those appeared frequently. Clubs and shields, goblets, and weapon bun-

dles — the weapons and clothing of defeated opponents — are common in Moro fineline paintings. Weapon bundles decorate the spouts of more than half of Moro stirrup spout bottles, and they surround or are associated with all depictions of Paddler in reed boat scenes [e.g., 3.1] and Supernatural Confrontation scenes [e.g., 3.54]. Around the chamber of the ceramic goblet in figure 2.10, the artist painted a row of anthropomorphized clubs, each of which is carrying a goblet. The female occupant of reed boats is sometimes portrayed holding a goblet [3.15–16], and an unusual bottle is decorated with anthropomorphized weapon bundles carrying goblets containing ulluchus (see p. 148) [3.119]. Weapon bundles separate some crescent boats [3.25]. A fineline painted sherd from Moro [3.120], two jars [2.23, 3.121], and two double spout and bridge bottles illustrate weapon bundles [2.12e, 3.122].

3.118 *Warfare scene painted with white slip on a red background.*

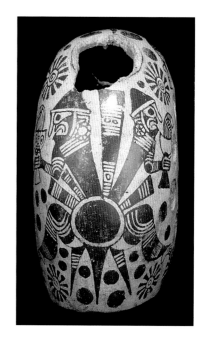

3.119 *Bottle with a doughnut-shaped chamber. Anthropomorphized weapon bundles hold goblets containing ulluchus.*

3.120   Sherd from Moro with
a painting of a weapon bundle.

3.121   Jar decorated with weapon bundles.
The rim is painted with Huari-derived chevrons.

3.122   Polychrome double spout and bridge
bottle illustrating Moche weapon bundles.

THE WAVED SPIRAL NARRATIVE

This narrative appears on a spout and handle bottle [3.123] and three stirrup spout bottles [3.124, 4.25–26].[29] At least three different activities are combined in a spiral layout: animated objects, reed boats, and the Sacrifice Ceremony. The curls on the spiral under the figures are wave motifs that indicate an ocean setting. Although no specific graphic elements separate the stages of the narration (as the double lines do in the Burial Theme), the passage of time can be inferred from the appearance of particular individuals and objects at several places along the spiral.

The sequence of the activities is the same on all four spirals, although the number of participants varies considerably. The direction of motion is clockwise (right to left) on the spout and handle bottle and counterclockwise on the three stirrup spout vessels, but the activities are always divided in the same way and arranged in the same relative positions, as in the Burial Theme. The consistent order of the four activities in the Waved Spiral Narration shows that they must be interrelated.

The reed boat paintings from Moro that depict Paddler and the female (see Reed Boats, p. 30) give us no way to determine which one the artist intended to be in front. However, the four vessels that depict Paddler and the female in their boats as part of the Waved Spiral Narrative indicate that Paddler leads the procession, followed by the female. In each of these four scenes, the female is followed by a third boat carrying an anthropomorphized animal (fox?) holding a weapon bundle and wearing a crescent headdress. So far, this figure appears only in these spiral narratives and not in individual reed boat depictions.

3.123 *Waved Spiral painting on a spout and handle bottle.*

The sequence begins at the bottom of the chamber with a group of animated objects, some of which fight human warriors.[30] In each painting, a seated male figure wearing a headdress with a crescent ornament is painted in negative against a rayed background. He looks toward the start of the spiral and seems to be watching the combat between the animated objects and the human warriors.

Farther up the spiral, a female figure stands in front of a structure filled with weapon bundles. She also looks toward the animated objects. In all of the paintings except one [3.124], the animated objects seem to be moving toward her.

Continuing up the spiral are three reed boats containing Paddler, followed by the female, followed by an animal warrior. Some of the boats carry containers, possibly gourds with handles, under their netted decks. These containers project above the deck of the boat in the animated objects group at the bottom of the spiral. Similar containers appear in almost every activity in the spiral. The boats arrive at another ritual structure where a part of the Sacrifice Ceremony is taking place. In front of the structure, an anthropomorphized club and shield holds a goblet. A bird faces a seated figure inside the structure, who also holds a goblet.[31] The female is seated behind the ritual structure. In the painting on the spout and handle bottle [3.123], there are two female figures at the top of the spiral facing each other with a bowl between them. One is seated holding a goblet and the other is standing.

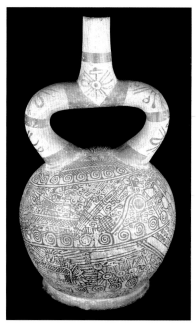

3.124 *Waved Spiral painting.*

COMBINED ACTIVITIES

SEVERAL MORO VESSELS COMBINE seemingly unrelated activities in the same painting. Scenes with combined activities may or may not be narratives. Of the five types of scenes in our Moro sample that illustrate combined activities, only the Waved Spiral Narrative has a clear narrative structure, indicated by the appearance of the same figure at more than one location in the scene.

The painting in figure 3.125 includes portions of several activities: the Warrior Narrative and Sacrifice Ceremony, musical processions, animated objects, and possibly the Burial Theme. It may represent a funeral procession. However, since it lacks repeated depictions of the same major figure, it does not appear to be a narrative.

The scene is separated by lines that spiral four times around the chamber. It depicts a long, continuous procession of groups of figures, including warriors, musicians, blind people, and an individual being carried in a litter.[32] In the midst of the procession are two structures. In one of the structures, a figure holds a goblet containing an ulluchu (see Plants, p. 146).

There are three humans with splayed legs. One is lying on his back across the top of the chamber and has an animal between his legs.

3.125 *Spiral painting of a complex procession.*

TWO ACTIVITIES SEEM TO MERGE in this unique painting [3.126]. The focus is on a portion of the Sacrifice Ceremony under the gabled-roof structure, but it is surrounded by animated objects. This is one of the most remarkable examples of animation. The artist added human and animal arms, legs, and heads to many objects, including jars, stacked gourds, headdresses, feathered capes, shells, war clubs, panpipes, and a drum.

3.126 Combined activities scene. Elements of the Sacrifice Ceremony surrounded by animated objects.

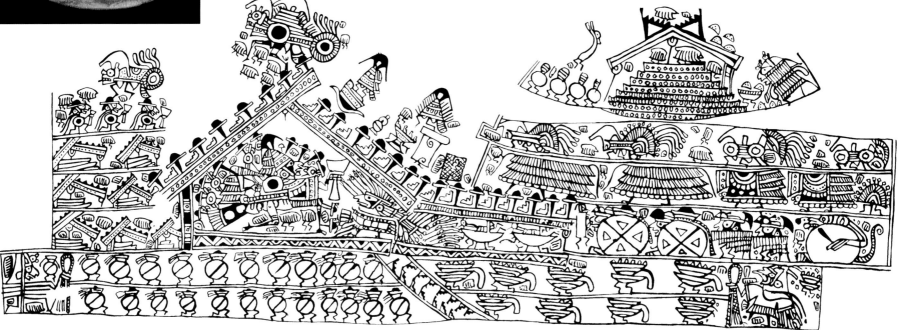

THE PAINTING IN FIGURE 3.127 depicts two subjects that at first glance seem unrelated: Paddler in his reed boat on one side of the chamber and a Supernatural Confrontation scene involving Wrinkle Face and the Anthropomorphized Wave on the other. Although we have no other vessels depicting this combination of activities, Paddler appears in several Supernatural Confrontation scenes (see p. 62).

3.127 *Painting combining a reed boat with Supernatural Confrontation.*

THE PAINTING IN FIGURE 3.128 has an Anthropomorphized Wave standing on its head on one side of the chamber and a large square frame on the other side. The frame is borne by several warriors carrying spear throwers. The warrior at the top also carries darts or spears. The figure in the center of the frame is holding a club and has plant elements (manioc?) attached to his clothing and body. A smaller, empty frame is carried by four warriors between the large frame and the Anthropomorphized Wave. On the opposite side of the chamber is a strange scene in which five individuals, one carrying a sling, run around a ring. Above the ring is a large scorpion. Natural and anthropomorphized sea anemones are in the background. They and the Anthropomorphized Wave suggest an ocean setting. On the spout is a scorpion, which, along with the remainder of the painted spout design, is unique in our Moro sample.

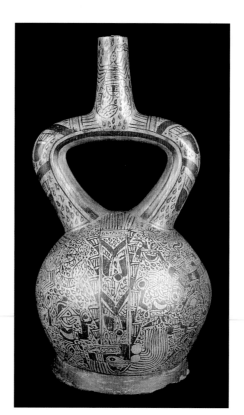

3.128 Combined activities scene.

OTHER MOCHE DEPICTIONS AT MORO

MORO ARTISTS DEPICTED A VARIETY of animals, plants, and abstract symbols. Many of these appear in complex scenes, but some are only shown as individual depictions.

ANIMALS

Many Moro fineline paintings depict two animal creatures.[33] Usually the same figure appears on each side of the chamber, but sometimes the two figures are different. In a few cases, multiple depictions of a natural animal encircle the chamber of a vessel [3.139, 3.142, 3.144–147].

Most Moro animal images are anthropomorphized or zoomorphized, but some are natural animals:

- *Anthropomorphized animals*: birds, crabs, crayfish, fish (Demon Fish), sea anemones, sea lions
- *Zoomorphized animal*: Strombus Monster
- *Natural animals*: birds, fish, octopuses, rays, sea anemones, sea lions, and spiders

Many of the animals are ocean dwellers or appear in Supernatural Confrontation, an ocean activity. This reflects the shift to marine settings and activities.[34]

Ocean Creatures. Six paintings feature Anthropomorphized Crabs [3.129–134]. All the crabs have triangular or trapezoidal carapaces.[35]

3.129   Anthropomorphized Crabs.

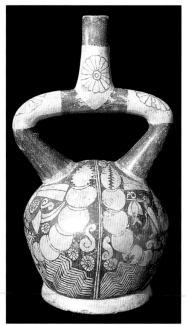

3.130 *Anthropomorphized Crabs.*

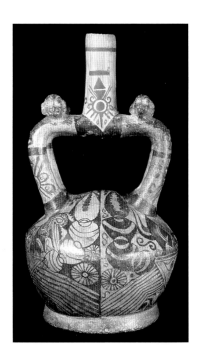

3.131 *Anthropomorphized Crabs. The upper spout has been restored.*

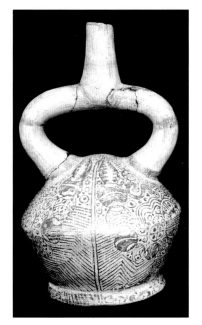

3.132 *Anthropomorphized Crabs.*

3.133 *(above)   Strombus Monster and Anthropomorphized Crab. .*

3.134 *(below)   Anthropomorphized Crab and Demon Fish.*

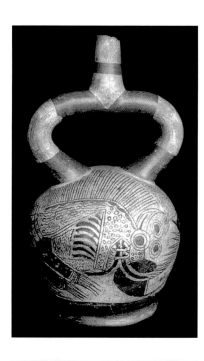

3.135 *Strombus Monsters.*

One depiction shows the Anthropomorphized Crab with a Strombus Monster [3.133] and another with a large, aggressive-looking fish holding a tumi, which we have named the Demon Fish [3.134].[36]

3.136 *Inverted Strombus Monsters.*

Two paintings portray only Strombus Monsters [3.135–136]. In one, the creatures are upside down.

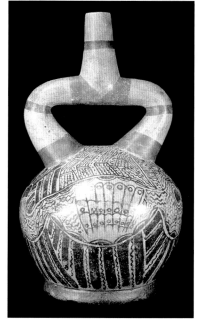

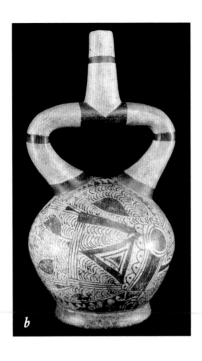

Three additional paintings feature Demon Fish [3.137]. Their tongues have an unusual pointed shape. A small fish resembling the Demon Fish, but without the pointed tongue and anthropomorphic attributes, is depicted in one painting, surrounded by beans and geometric designs [3.138].

ALTHOUGH THERE IS NO MORO IMAGE of an octopus located in an ocean setting, natural octopuses are repeated around the chamber of one vessel [3.139].

3.137 *Demon Fish.*

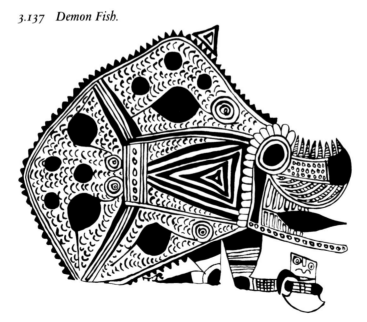

3.138   *Fish, beans, and geometric designs on a sharply angled chamber.*

3.139   *Natural octopuses.*

SEA ANEMONES WITH FACES are featured on two vessels [3.140–141].

SEA LIONS WEARING HEADDRESSES AND SASHES are painted on two jars [3.142–143]. Both jars have Huari-style chevrons around their rims. One is a face-neck jar with a supernatural face. An exam-

3.140 *Sea anemones with faces.*

3.141 *Sea anemones with faces.*

ple of the lobed vessel form has sea lions wearing headdresses on the cylindrical part of the chamber [3.144]. Objects resembling fish tails are painted below on the six lobes.[37] There is an unidentified circular shape on the arch of the spout (seen at the right of the drawing). It may represent a marine animal. The short jutting lines outlining the figure resemble cilia. Seven of these curious

3.142   *Jar depicting anthropomorphized sea lions. Note Huari-style chevrons on rim.*

3.143   *Face-neck jar depicting anthropomorphized sea lions. Note Huari-style chevrons on rim.*

3.144 *Lobed stirrup spout vessel depicting anthropomorphized sea lions.*

shapes are featured on a jar [3.145]. A white-on-red painting on a stirrup spout bottle illustrates several bands of sea lions surrounding the upper half of the angled chamber [3.146]. The

3.145 *Jar depicting the unidentified creature shown at the right-hand end of the drawing in figure 3.144. Note Huari-style chevrons on rim.*

white or black circles in front of the sea lions' mouths in several of these paintings may also represent stomach stones [3.142–144, 3.146].[38]

A CREATURE FOUND ONLY in Moro fineline paintings appears to have a birdlike head and beak, wings, and a forked tail, but no legs. In two scenes [3.130, 3.147], these creatures are being held in the beaks of large birds. They also appear alone in the back-

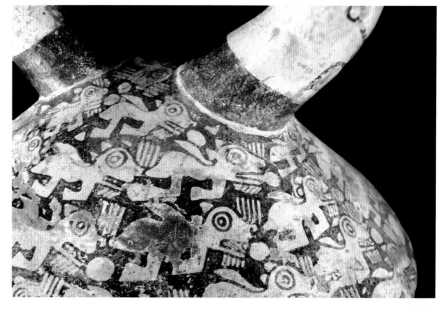

3.146 *White-on-red design depicting sea lions on sharply angled chamber.*

3.147 *Birds with flying fish (?) in their beaks.*

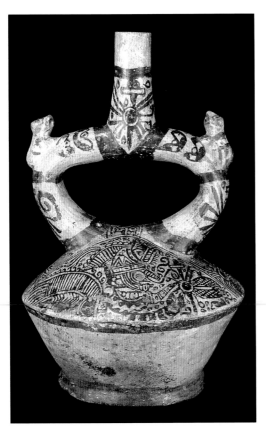

ground of an Anthropomorphized Crab painting [3.133] and in a wave arching over the female figure in a crescent boat scene [3.24]. They may be flying fish, which are common off the coast of Peru.[39] On seeing flying fish swim under water and then "fly" for great distances, the Moche may have viewed them as part bird and part fish and added a beak to create a bird-fish combination.

OUR SAMPLE CONTAINS FOUR PAINTINGS of crayfish warriors: [3.148–150, 4.20]. Each of the warriors is holding a weapon bundle. The warriors in figure 3.148 appear to be Wrinkle Face, based on their headdresses, clothing, and facial lines.

3.148 *Wrinkle Face (?) as a crayfish warrior.*

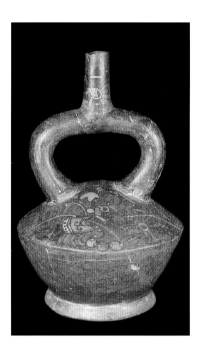

3.149 *Polychrome painting of crayfish warriors.*

3.150 *Crayfish warriors.*

a Supernatural Confrontation (detail of figure 3.60).

b Ceremonial Badminton (detail of figure 3.92).

c Burial Theme (detail of figure 3.103).

d Combined activities (detail of figure 3.126).

e Combined activities (detail of figure 3.125).

3.151 Depiction of shells in Moro paintings.

3.152 **Spondylus** *shell.*

SHELLS ARE PROMINENT in five types of Moro depictions [3.151]. Only one of these, Supernatural Confrontation, has an ocean setting. The significance of shells in land settings is not clear. Many of the shells appear to be conch (*Strombus*), which are widely depicted in Moche art. The shell depictions with more generic shapes are probably also conch.

Another type of shell, the *Spondylus* or spiny oyster [3.152],[40] is extremely rare in Moche art, In our sample, it is depicted in only one painting — a frontal-facing monster bedecked with snakes [3.153]. Its hands and feet are snake heads, and it is surrounded by *Spondylus* shells.

3.153 *Spondylus Monster.*

Birds. Eight paintings feature birds. One portrays bird decapitators who hold a human head in one hand and a tumi in the other [3.154].[41] Four other paintings feature bird warriors [3.155–156]. In three of these, the birds are Muscovy ducks [3.155].

One painting portrays birds that appear to float on water [3.157]. Another portrays a crested bird [3.158], and the third shows an anthropomorphized bird holding a goblet [3.159).

3.154   Bird decapitator.

3.155 *Muscovy duck warriors.*

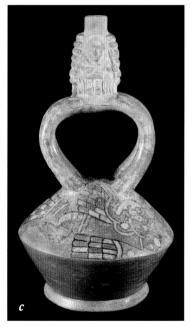

3.156 *Bird warriors.*

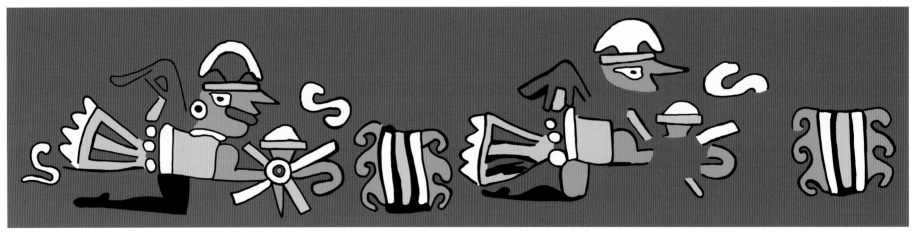

3.157 *Birds appearing to float on water.*

3.158 *Crested bird.*

3.159 *Anthropomorphized bird holding a goblet.*

Insects and Spiders. Although many insects were anthropomorphized in paintings from the Southern Moche Region, we have found only a single example at Moro [3.160].

Spiders appear frequently in ocean settings between the crescent boats in which the female sits [3.27–28][42] and between crayfish warriors [3.148]. One painting portrays a spider at the top of the chamber surrounded by hanging bird heads. Spiders encircle the upper half of the chamber inside a band with serrated borders [3.161]. All spider depictions at Moro are naturalistic.

The association of spiders with the ocean may result from the abundance of ground spiders and their silk-lined tunnels on nearly all of the Peruvian islands. The spiders provide food for the guano birds.[43] The Moche may have observed these spiders and their tunnels when they went to the islands.

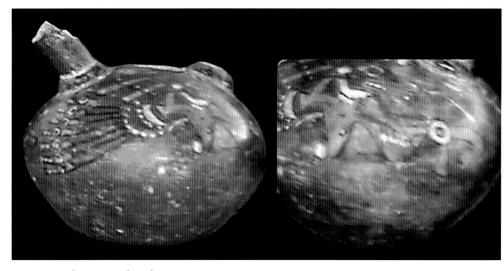

3.160 Anthropomorphized insect warrior.

3.161 Spiders encircling a double spout and bridge bottle.

PLANTS

The plants depicted in Moro paintings — beans, ulluchus, and manioc — have been in the Moche inventory since earlier phases in the Southern Moche Region. Beans are the most common plants. They appear in the background of complex fineline paintings, but the greatest number fill the space around the figures in the Bean and Stick Ceremony [e.g., 3.72].

Manioc is often associated with beans. One painting shows two standing figures, each on a dais with manioc tubers and beans [3.162]. The daises, beans, and manioc suggest a land location. Other aspects of the scene, however, suggest an ocean setting: the net-covered steps on the daises resemble the decks of reed boats, the net balls on one rope are similar to those attached

3.162   Figures with plant attributes. The painting has both land and sea associations.

to reed boats, S-shaped wave symbols are in the background, and the daises are separated by sea anemones. Both figures wear headdresses similar to those usually worn by Wrinkle Face in Supernatural Confrontation, the Bean and Stick Ceremony, Ceremonial Badminton, and the Burial Theme.

The association between beans and manioc is manifested in a different way in figure 3.163. Two standing figures hold double-headed serpent ropes arching over their heads. Manioc tubers splay out from the ropes. More manioc tubers surround the standing figures. Between the standing figures are two anthropomorphized sea anemones with manioc tubers replacing their tentacles. A few beans are in the background. The faces of the two figures are similar to those in the De Vault paintings (p. 82).

3.163   *Two figures with plant attributes in the style of the De Vault paintings.*

See 3.94

Agricultural deities modeled on the spout in figure 3.164 hold corn stalks and clusters of manioc tubers above frogs resting on the double arches. The arches are covered with beans.

THE ULLUCHU IS A GROOVED, comma-shaped object with an enlarged calyx. In Moro paintings, ulluchus are often carried in goblets [3.165a].[44] They are in one of the Moro Burial Theme paintings [3.165b], and they appear in the background of runners [3.165c]. The significance of the ulluchu is unknown, but its prevalence in Moche art strongly suggests that it conveyed an important symbolic meaning.[45]

3.164 *Modeled agricultural deities on upper spout.*

3.165 *Ulluchus in Moro paintings.*

a *Warrior Narrative (detail of figure 3.119).*

b *Burial Theme (detail of figure 3.113).*

c *Ritual Running (detail of figure 3.99).*

Until recently, we were uncertain whether the ulluchu was a real or a mythical plant; however, the remains of actual ulluchus [3.166] have been archaeologically excavated at two sites.[46] Two Moro vessels, one decorated in low relief [3.167] and the other in polychrome paint [3.168], show monkeys in trees gathering ulluchus.

3.166 *Archaeologically excavated ulluchu (length 2.9 cm).*

3.167 *Low-relief vessel depicting monkeys gathering ulluchus from trees.*

3.168 *Polychrome vessel depicting*
monkeys gathering ulluchus from trees.

GEOMETRIC DESIGNS

In contrast to painted vessels from the Southern Moche Region,[47] vessels from Moro were seldom painted with geometric designs. Our Moro sample contains only two examples. One of the two was excavated at Moro [3.169a]. The high-set position of the stirrup spout on the chamber is typical of vessels from the Southern Moche Region, but the ring base is more characteristic of vessels from Moro. The other vessel comes from a grave-lot at the site of Cenicero (PV28-97) in the Santa Valley [3.169b].[48]

3.169 Moro vessels with geometric designs.

HUARI-DERIVED DESIGNS

Huari ceramics introduced new designs to Moro artists. A popular new motif, seemingly unrelated to anything in Moche art, is the volute [2.12b, 2.14a, 3.170–180, 3.182–183],[49] which appears in a variety of designs. One of the most common is the double-headed diamond, which has volutes emanating from it.

3.170 Double spout and bridge bottle with double-headed diamonds and volutes.

3.171 *Double spout and bridge bottle with double-headed diamonds and volutes.*

3.172 *Double spout and bridge bottle with double-headed diamonds and volutes.*

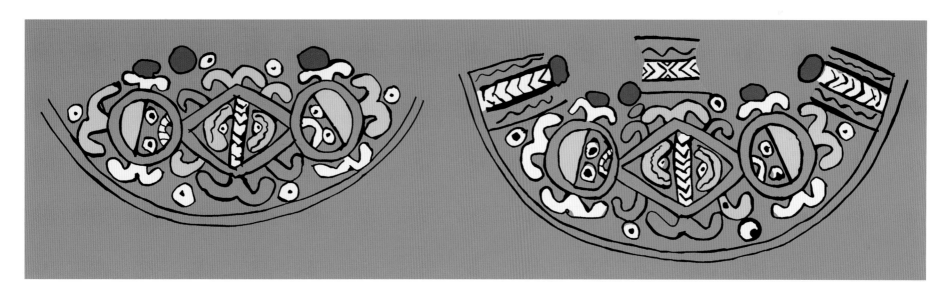

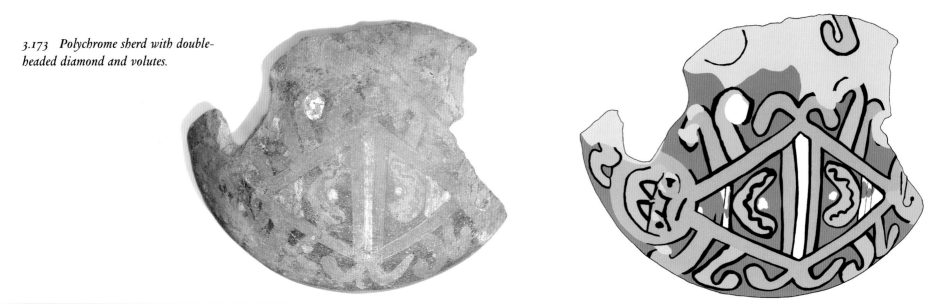

3.173 *Polychrome sherd with double-headed diamond and volutes.*

3.174 *Double spout and bridge bottle with double-headed diamonds and volutes.*

Although most examples of the double-headed diamond design are found on double spout and bridge bottles, they were also painted on Moche stirrup spout bottles [3.175–176]. The stirrup spout vessel in figure 3.177 has an abstracted version of the double-headed diamond.

3.175 *Stirrup spout bottle with double-headed diamonds and volutes.*

3.176 *Stirrup spout bottle with double-headed diamonds and volutes.*

3.177 *Stirrup spout bottle with double-headed serpent on the arch. The design on the chamber is an abstracted version of the double-headed diamond.*

3.178 *Cup with double-headed serpent and volutes.*

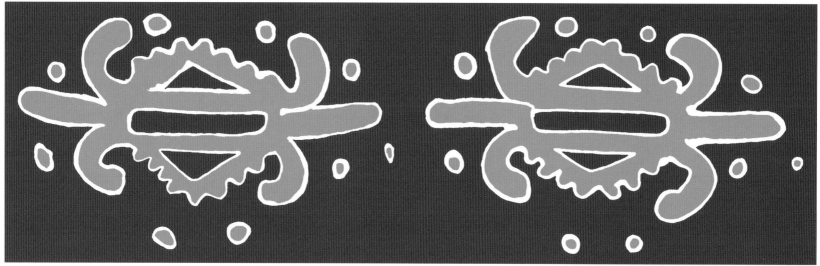

On two polychrome painted cups, a sinuous double-headed animal with volutes encircles the chamber [2.14a, 3.178].[50]

A Moche-Huari blend appears on a double spout and bridge bottle [3.179]. The chamber is painted in polychrome with a Moche design of hanging heads; however, volutes were added to their mouths.

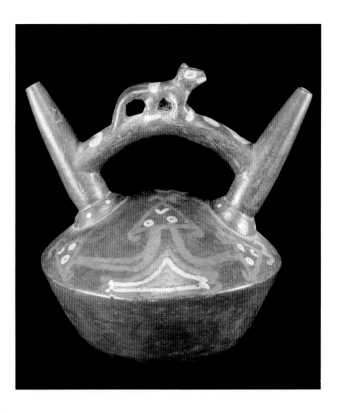

3.179 *Double spout and bridge bottle with hanging heads and volutes.*

3.180 Six-lobed double spout and bridge vessel with double-headed insect.

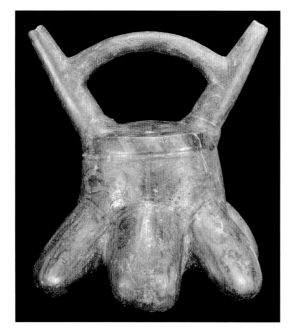

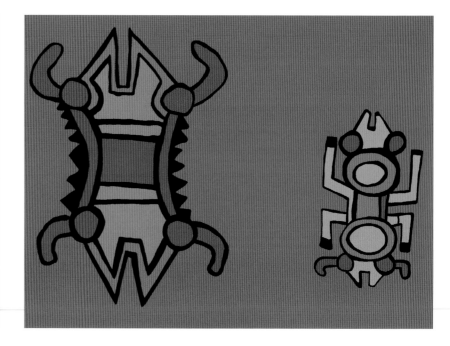

3.181 Six-lobed double spout and bridge vessel with chevrons and "open 8" motifs.

Two six-lobed polychrome vessels appear to have Huari-derived designs. One has double-headed insects on the top of the chamber and on the lobes [3.180]. The other was painted with a Moche "open 8" design on the top of chamber and on the lobes [3.181].

3.182   Pod-shaped vessel with volutes.

Our sample contains two pod-shaped vessels with cylindrical necks [3.182–183].[51] The design painted on each is an elongated "S" with volutes.[52]

3.183   Pod-shaped vessel with volutes.

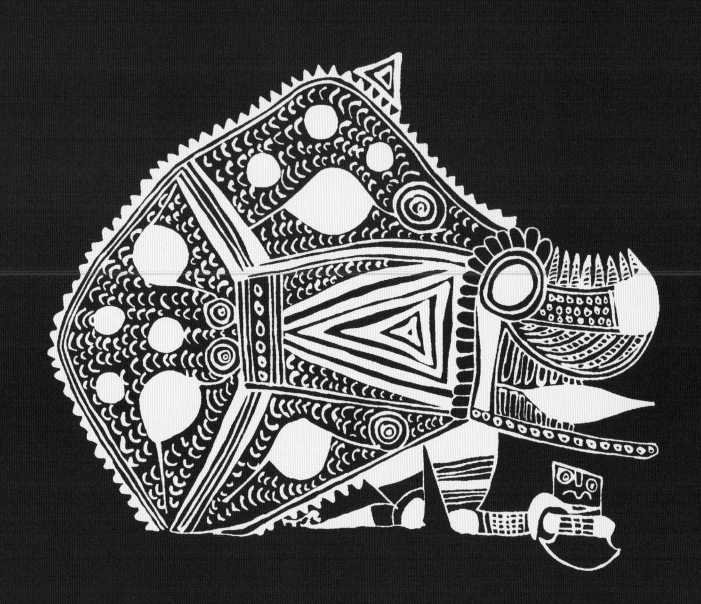

4 The Moro Artists

WITHIN OUR SAMPLE of fineline painted vessels from Moro, we have been able to identify multiple paintings by individual artists. The unique style in which an artist paints is as distinctive as a person's handwriting. The easiest way of recognizing an artist's style is to examine the way he portrayed anatomical features: the shape and position of the eyes, chin, nose, mouth, arms, hands, feet, legs, and shoulders, and the overall proportions and posture of the figure. Other elements such as clothing, background objects, and brush strokes may also be useful. Usually, several of these factors must be used to determine that two paintings are by the same artist.[1]

When we published *Moche Fineline Painting* in 1999, we had identified six Moro artists for whom we could recognize more than one painting: the Amano Painter, the Moro Painter, the Rodriguez Painter, the Burial Theme Painter, the Large Lip Painter, and the Reed Boat Painter.[2]

Since the publication of MFP, we have identified twelve more artists from Moro. In this chapter, we will describe the characteristics of their work and illustrate their paintings.

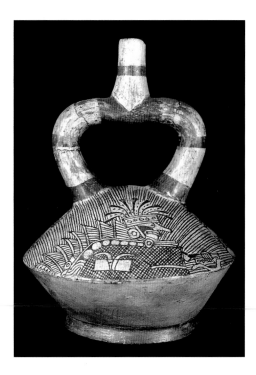

THE CRESCENT BOAT PAINTER — There are eight paintings by this artist [4.1–8], two of which were excavated at Moro [4.2, 4.6]. All are on stirrup spout bottles with angled chambers. Each of them features female figures in crescent boats. Since the paintings all illustrate the same subject, the sample offers an opportunity to study the range of variation in the work of one artist. The angled

4.1   *The Crescent Boat Painter.*

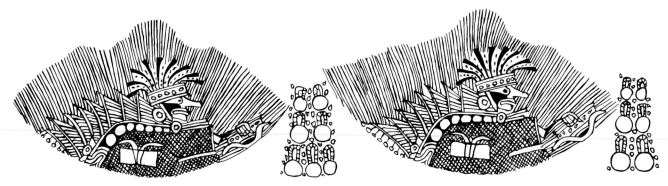

4.2   *The Crescent Boat Painter.*

equator serves as the boat on four of the vessels [4.1–4], while the crescent is painted on the other four [4.5–8]. Each of the female figures has an elongated nose. The mouths are outlined with a white band and the chins are white. In most cases, the lips protrude as thin lines. All the boats are surrounded by lines. In seven of the eight paintings, the boats are separated by objects, including containers [4.1–4], a ray [4.5], or wave symbols [4.7–8]. The other painting [4.6] has no separators. Each female has a tied rectangular bundle near her waist and holds a textile-wrapped container in front of her. Several females hold a spatula or chisel in their forward hand (see p. 33).

4.3   *The Crescent Boat Painter.*

4.4   *The Crescent Boat Painter.*

4.5 *The Crescent Boat Painter.*

4.6 *The Crescent Boat Painter*

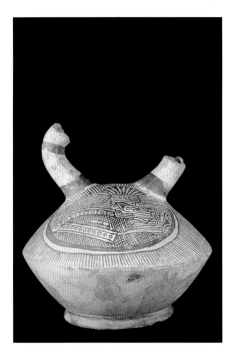

4.7 *The Crescent Boat Painter.*

4.8 *The Crescent Boat Painter.*

THE ELITE FEMALE PAINTER — We have identified two nearly identical paintings by this painter [4.9–10]. They are on stirrup spout bottles with sharply angled equators. The female figure sits in a crescent boat, which is represented by the sharp equator of the chamber. Although there are minor differences between these paintings, the distinctive sharply pointed nose, the gap between the upper lip and nose, and the raised arm indicate that these vessels are by the same artist.

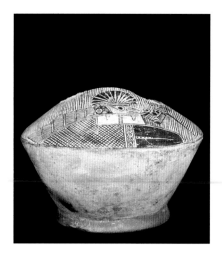

4.9 *The Elite Female Painter.*

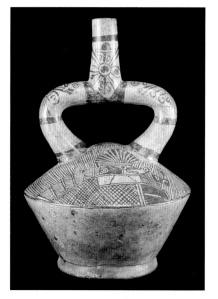

4.10 *The Elite Female Painter.*

THE GAPING MOUTH PAINTER — The two paintings we have identified by the Gaping Mouth Painter are on differently shaped stirrup spout bottles. Both portray the female figure in a crescent boat [4.11–12]. The rounded mouth of the female has a fat upper lip and gapes open. The entire top of the eye is juxtaposed to the headdress, the cheek paint curves back, and the headdress stands upright in front. The ends of the crescent boat are rounded, and the lines within the crescent are nearly horizontal.

4.11 *The Gaping Mouth Painter.*

4.12 *The Gaping Mouth Painter.*

THE DOWN IN THE MOUTH PAINTER — The drooping mouths of the figures on two differently shaped chambers identify the works by this painter [4.13–14]. Both depict boat scenes, one with reed boats and the other with crescent boats. On one bottle, the female figure and Paddler each occupy a reed boat. On the other, the female is in both of the crescent boats. In both types of boat, her body is reduced to a partial circle with no legs or arms. The faces of Paddler and the female have pulled-back eyes and drooping noses.

Although these two paintings are very similar to those of the

4.13   The Down in the Mouth Painter: reed boats.

Gaping Mouth Painter, they seem to be by a different artist. A comparison of the characteristics listed above discloses numerous differences: the headdress does not stand upright in front, the mouth turns down at the back and does not gape, the top of the pulled-back eye is not continuously adjacent to the headdress, and the crescent boat ends are pointed. In addition, the body shape of the female in the crescent boat [4.14] is a flatter arc than either of the paintings by the Gaping Mouth Painter. Despite the discrepancies, it is likely that the two artists were familiar with each other's work.

4.14   The Down in the Mouth Painter: crescent boats.

THE ANTHROPOMORPHIZED WAVE PAINTER — This artist painted at least three vessels featuring the Anthropomorphized Wave. Two of the paintings are almost identical, with Wrinkle Face fighting the Anthropomorphized Wave and the Strombus Monster [4.15–16]. One is on a false jar neck stirrup spout bottle and the other is on a stirrup spout bottle with a sharply angled chamber. The hair on the figure under the wave balloons forward distinctively. The third painting is on a sherd excavated at Moro.

4.15 The Anthropomorphized Wave Painter: Supernatural Confrontation between Wrinkle Face, the Anthropomorphized Wave, and Strombus Monster.

Although it includes only the isolated head of the Anthropomorphized Wave, it is painted by the same hand as the two whole vessels [4.17].

4.16 (left) The Anthropomorphized Wave Painter: Supernatural Confrontation between Wrinkle Face, the Anthropomorphized Wave, and Strombus Monster.

4.17 (below) Sherd from Moro by the Anthropomorphized Wave Painter.

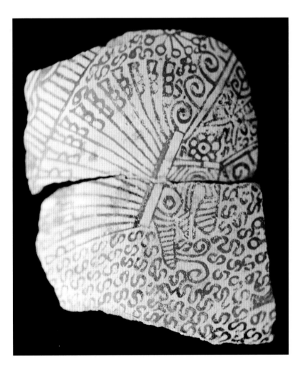

THE TENDRIL MOUTH PAINTER — This artist painted on the upper half of the angled chambers of three bottles. Two of the bottles portray the female figure sitting in a crescent boat [4.18–19]. In figure 4.18, the two females are not identical; only one wears a dotted neck scarf. The torsos and legs of both females are depicted, but they are rendered as an extreme example of the U-shaped torso position.[3] The female portrayed on the other vessel is different — she has a scarf decorated with an undulating stripe, and an armless and legless body [4.19]. In figure 4.18, the artist used the sharply angled equator to repre-

4.18   *The Tendril Mouth Painter.*

4.19   *The Tendril Mouth Painter.*

sent the crescent boat, but he painted the actual crescent in figure 4.19. The third painting by the Tendril Mouth Painter depicts crayfish warriors [4.20].

In all of the paintings by this artist, a fairly wide band outlines the lips of the figures, and they have noses that look as if they have been pulled out to a thin drooping line. A thin tendril also issues from the upper lips, and the crayfish warriors have tendrils on the ends of their noses.

4.20   The Tendril Mouth Painter: crayfish warriors.

THE BEAN AND STICK PAINTER — The two paintings by this artist are on vessels with very similar chambers, spouts, and bridges [4.21–22]. They are both painted with scenes of the Bean and Stick Ceremony, in which Wrinkle Face and Iguana hold sticks. Although these two figures are usually portrayed lying prone on top of daises, this artist painted them above the curved equator of the chamber, which he used to represent the tops of the daises. This is analogous to the crescent boat scenes in which the boat is not painted, but is represented by the curved equator of the chamber.

4.21 *The Bean and Stick Painter.*

Despite the similarity of these vessels and the paintings on them, both figures in figure 4.21 are Wrinkle Face, while at least one of the figures in the painting in figure 4.22 is Iguana. The face of the other figure in that painting is mostly obliterated, but he is wearing Wrinkle Face's typical headdress. The shirt patterns on the figures in the two paintings are virtually identical.

4.22 The Bean and Stick Painter.

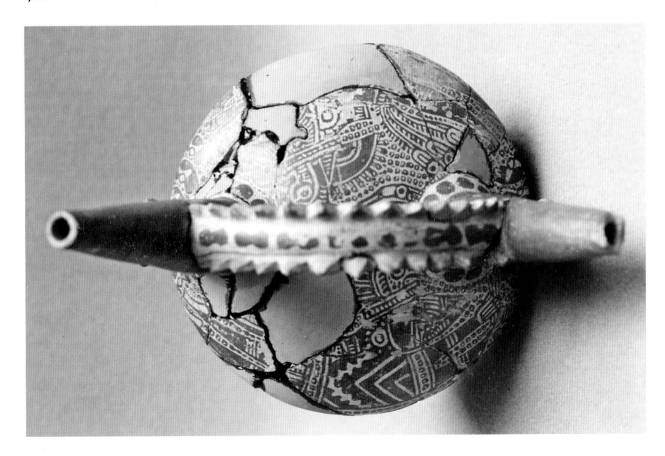

THE BRUJO PAINTER — One of the two paintings by this artist was found at the site of El Brujo in the Chicama Valley [4.23]. For this reason, we have named him the Brujo Painter. Nevertheless, the chamber shapes, double spouts, and modeled spout decorations of these vessels strongly suggest that they were produced at Moro.[4] Although they depict different activities, Ceremonial Badminton [4.23] and Supernatural Confrontation [4.24], the great similarity of painting style marks them as the work of one artist. There is no mistaking the resemblance between the faces and the clothing decorations of the human figures. Also, the hands of the

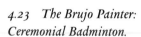

4.23 The Brujo Painter: Ceremonial Badminton.

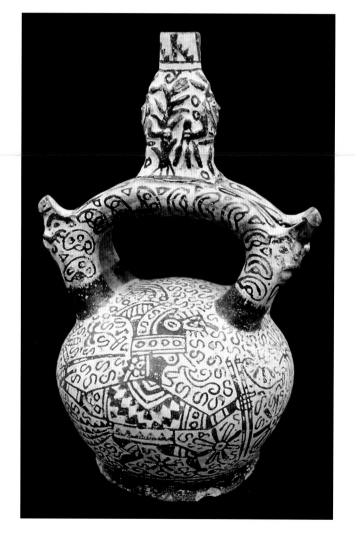

human figures do not seem to hide the outlines of the objects they are grasping. Both vessels are associated with agriculture. Beans are painted on the stirrup spouts of both vessels. The artist includes a figure surrounded by manioc as one of the combatants in the Supernatural Confrontation scene [4.24] (compare with figure 3.163). This figure may be Sea Urchin with its spines replaced by manioc tubers. The artist portrayed the Anthropomorphized Wave in an unusual way: a wave emanates from the anthropomorphized fox's head and another wave is attached to his back by a fish head inside the wave.

4.24   The Brujo Painter: Supernatural Confrontation between Wrinkle Face, the Anthropomorphized Wave, and Sea Urchin.

THE WAVED SPIRAL PAINTER — Two of the four paintings of the Waved Spiral Narrative [4.25–26] are by the same artist, as is clear from the faces, the positions of many of the figures, and the "stick figure" appearance of the animated objects. Although both show the same sequence of four activities, these complex paintings reveal how one artist varied his rendering of the same scene.

While one painting [4.25] has twenty-five participants on the spiral, the other [4.26] has only fifteen. The element at the beginning of the spiral in both paintings resembles a circular ear ornament with the attached rod that goes through the ear lobe. If these are ear ornaments, they are the only examples we have of isolated ear ornaments in fineline painting.

4.25 *The Waved Spiral Painter.*

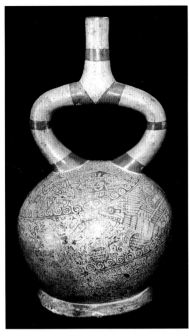

The vessel in figure 4.26 is heavily spalled, but we were able to identify its missing images by locating them in the other roll-out drawing [4.25]. We moved those images (the grayed areas) from figure 4.25 to figure 4.26 to show how the original painting may have looked.

4.26 *The Waved Spiral Painter. The rollout drawing has been reconstructed from parts of figure 4.25.*

THE MOON PAINTER — Two nearly identical vessels display a female figure inside a deeply curved crescent boat [4.27–28]. Serpent-headed rays emanate from the boat and the female. In all aspects of painting style, vessel shape, and slip color, these two vessels are among the most similar in our entire sample of Moche art.

4.27 The Moon Painter.

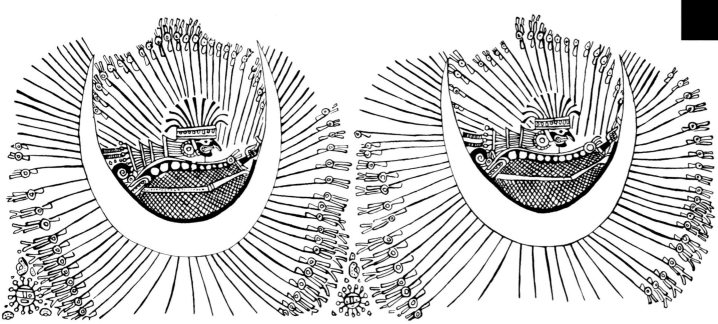

4.28 The Moon Painter.

THE HOOK NOSE PAINTER — The four paintings by this artist are boat scenes on stirrup spout bottles. Three show the female figure in a crescent boat on an angled chamber [4.29–31]. The other shows reed boats carrying the female on one side and Paddler on the other side of a round chamber [4.32]. The individu-als on all four bottles share a hooked nose, pointed chin, pulled back eye form, and the same placement of the ear ornament rel-ative to the headdress. The circular shoulder ornament on the female also has the same placement.

4.29   The Hook Nose Painter: crescent boats.

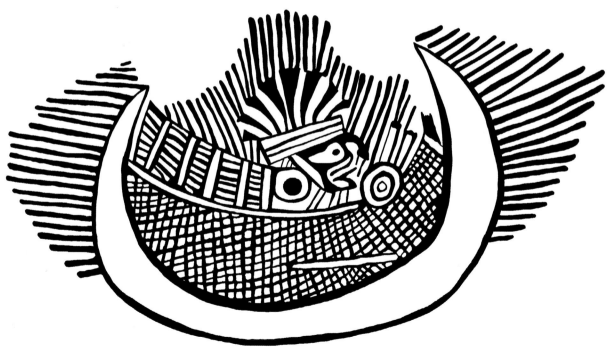

4.30 *The Hook Nose Painter: crescent boats.*   4.31 *The Hook Nose Painter: crescent boats.*   4.32 *The Hook Nose Painter: reed boats.*

THE PENDANT NOSE PAINTER — This artist painted the same figures, Wrinkle Face and Circular Creature, engaged in Supernatural Confrontation on two vessels [4.33–34]. All the figures have long pendant noses.

4.33 *The Pendant Nose Painter: Supernatural Confrontation between Wrinkle Face and the Circular Creature.*

*4.34   The Pendant Nose Painter: Supernatural Confrontation
between Wrinkle Face and the Circular Creature.*

5 Conclusions

MORO ARTISTS CREATED a unique fineline painting style that is distinguishable from the fineline painting of the Southern Moche Region. In the Southern Moche Region, there had been a gradual evolution in fineline painted vessels between Phase I and Phase IV. Then, in Phase V, there was a dramatic departure from this trajectory. Of the many vessel forms that had been painted in previous phases, only flaring bowls and stirrup spout bottles continued to be decorated in this way. Moreover, the inventory of activities that had been depicted in previous phases was dramatically reduced in Phase V. Although some excellent fineline painted ceramics were still being produced, the painting tradition in the Southern Moche Region appears to have lost a great deal of the vigor and momentum that characterized its earlier development.

Meanwhile, the first significant production of fineline painted vessels in the Northern Moche Region began. It was centered at San José de Moro, where the production of fineline painted vessels exhibits a remarkable degree of innovation and creativity. No precedent for the painting at Moro has been found in the Northern Moche Region, but Moro artists often depicted the same complex themes and activities as their southern counterparts. Thus, although their style was new, the objects and activities they illustrated were derived from Moche fineline painting in the south. Moro artists continued to paint on several vessel forms that had previously been used in the south, as well as on new vessel forms, such as the flask and the goblet.

Moreover, the potters and painters at San José de Moro borrowed three features from the Huari ceramic tradition: vessel forms (including double spout and bridge bottles, cups, and pod-shaped vessels), polychrome slip painting, and design motifs.[1] They combined these new features with Moche vessel forms, painting techniques, and design motifs. The combinations, along with innovations in layout, subject matter, and narrative techniques, resulted in an amazing diversity of fineline painted vessels, suggesting that the potters and painters at Moro were freely experimenting with the potentialities of their trade.

THE MORO SUBSTYLE OF MOCHE CERAMICS

IN THE SOUTHERN MOCHE REGION there had been a gradual increase in the degree of natural depiction from Phase I through Phase IV. By the end of Phase IV, most artists were painting in a very realistic way; their depictions of both humans and animals were remarkably lifelike. This natural depiction continued to characterize most of the paintings produced in the Southern Moche Region during Phase V.

In the Northern Moche Region, however, the Late Moche paintings at San José de Moro were more abstract. In portraying humans, the arms, legs, hands, and feet were often distorted; mouths were misshapen; and long noses were awkwardly appended to the forehead. The arms, torsos, and legs of many seated figures were reduced to a U shape [3.36][2] or replaced by a dome shape [4.11–13], which would be unrecognizable without seeing the earlier, more naturalistic representations. The depictions of animals and supernatural creatures by Moro painters

were also abstract and distorted, particularly when compared to their depiction by painters in the Southern Moche Region.

One might suggest that the Moro painters were simply not as skilled as their southern counterparts, and thus were unable to achieve the same degree of naturalism. Yet the amount of distortion suggests that there was a conscious effort by Moro painters to depict figures in a heavily stylized manner, as though they were deliberately trying to make their painting style different from that of their contemporaries in the south. This effort to produce a different style is also suggested by the weapon bundles they often painted on stirrup spouts — a motif that is not used on stirrup spouts in the Southern Moche Region.

In addition to the distinctive elements of Moro fineline painting, the potters at Moro may have deliberately created distinctive new chamber forms, some apparently borrowed from Huari and some innovated locally. Moro stirrup spouts tend to have characteristic shapes and proportions that set them apart from the stirrup spouts produced in the Southern Moche Region, as does their elaboration with modeled plants, animals, and human figures. All this suggests that the potters and painters at Moro were aware of the unique qualities of what they were producing, and were intentionally creating a distinctive substyle of Moche ceramics — one that would be recognizable not only to Moro people but also to people living outside the Moro region. Although present evidence does not allow us to understand how the Moro substyle developed, we believe that one of its functions was to demonstrate the ethnicity of the Moro polity.

DISTRIBUTION OF THE
MORO SUBSTYLE

A FEW EXAMPLES OF MORO-STYLE fineline painted vessels have been found outside of Moro. At the site of Pacatnamú, located approximately twenty-five kilometers from San José de Moro [1.2], several ceramic fragments have been found that appear to be from Moro-style fineline painted vessels.[3]

Outside of the Jequetepeque Valley, one stirrup spout bottle [3.169b] has been reported from the site of Cenicero (PV28-97) in the Santa Valley[4] and another [4.23] from the site of El Brujo in the Chicama Valley. A sherd from a Moro vessel [3.106] was found at Huaca Facho in the Lambayeque Valley.[5] Several examples of De Vault bottles have been found as far north as Piura[6] and as far south as the Rimac Valley[7] (see Polychrome Paintings and the De Vault Bottle Group, p. 82).

More examples of Moro-style fineline painted ceramics will be needed before it will be possible to suggest how the Moro polity was connected to other places, but it is hoped that this volume, by providing a detailed description of the Moro substyle, will serve to explore this aspect of Moche civilization as more evidence becomes available.

EPILOGUE

AT THE END OF PHASE V in the Southern Moche Region and the late Moche tradition at Moro in the Northern Moche Region, Moche fineline painting, along with Moche civilization, came to an end. The cause of this is not well understood. Suggested causes include natural disasters such as an intense El Niño resulting in severe damage to the Moche infrastructure, political upheavals, or simply replacement of the Moche artistic tradition by what may have seemed at the time to be innovative techniques and motifs.

Whatever the cause, by around A.D. 800 Moche civilization came to an end, and the complex Moche fineline painting style at Moro in the Northern Moche Region ended with it. The cultures that followed the Moche — Lambayeque in the northern region and Chimú in the southern region — continued to produce decorated ceramics, but their ceramics no longer exhibited the complex iconography, nor did they convey the intricate narratives that characterized Moro fineline painting.[8]

The legacy of Moche fineline painting at Moro can be traced into Lambayeque and Chimú. The Anthropomorphized Wave and a few other motifs can be seen in Lambayeque metalwork on double spout and bridge bottles[9] and tall, flaring cups [5.1]. The Anthropomorphized Wave is one of the most prevalent low-relief motifs in Chimú art [5.2]. In addition, the rare Moro fineline painting of a monster surrounded by *Spondylus* shells [3.153] foretells the importance of these shells in Lambayeque art, where they were portrayed in ceramics and metal.[10] The folded-leg position of an individual seated on a dais was also carried forward and can be recognized in a sculptured Lambayeque supernatural drummer seated on a dais [5.3].

THE NEW FORMS AND PAINTINGS that have come from the continuing excavations at Moro demonstrate the creativity of the Moro artists. Although we have photographed a large number of Moro vessels, we have not yet captured all of their diversity. The enigmatic scenes that we have referred to as combined activities suggest that the subjects we have identified, such as boats, Supernatural Confrontation, musical processions, or animated objects, may be parts of larger narratives that would have been recognized by Moche people. Within their limited range of subjects, Moro artists left us a unique legacy of late Moche art.

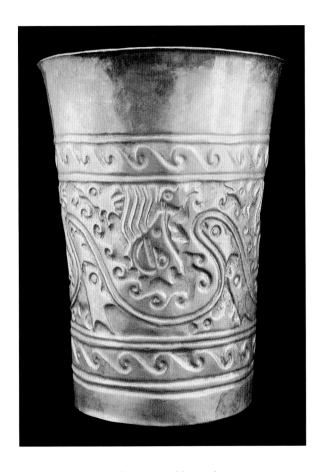

5.1 *Lambayeque gold cup depicting the Anthropomorphized Wave.*

5.2 *Chimu ceramic vessel depicting the Anthropomorphized Wave.*

5.3 *Lambayeque ceramic vessel showing the folded-leg seated position.*

Notes

PREFACE

1 Donnan and McClelland 1999: 9–23, 297. We have used the term "fineline paintings" to refer to the original Moche paintings on the ceramic vessels, and the term "rollout drawings" to refer to flat reproductions of those paintings. During our research we have identified figures that seem to represent specific individuals with well-defined roles in the fineline painted scenes. They have capitalized names, such as Wrinkle Face, to differentiate them from more generic participants, such as anthropomorphized birds. We have also identified certain scenes and themes that are repeated frequently with little variation. These also bear capitalized names, such as the Burial Theme, to set them apart from generic scenes such as musical processions. As in the 1999 book, we confine ourselves largely to description and illustration rather than interpretation of Moro art.

CHAPTER 1   INTRODUCTION

1 Donnan 1990, 1997; Castillo and Donnan 1994.

2 Donnan and McClelland 1999: 139.

3 Narvaez 1994; Donnan 2001, n.d.

4 Cock 1985.

5 Numerous vessel photographs in Chapters 1 and 2 (and figure 3.58 in Chapter 3) are repeated in Chapters 3 and 4 with the rollout drawings of their paintings, if available (see Sources of Illustrations, p. 196.)

6 Disselhoff (1956, 1957, 1958) investigated Moro in 1955–1956. Chodoff (1979) also excavated the site in the late 1970s.

7 For a comprehensive description of the excavations at Moro, see Castillo 2001.

8 Donnan and McClelland 1999: 131, 178.

9 Donnan 1977: 408; Donnan and McClelland 1999: 131. The Sacrifice Ceremony has also been called the Presentation Theme.

10 Broken ceramics were sometimes drilled with holes to tie pieces together and to prevent further breakage. This suggests that the bottles were valued and used even when broken.

11 See Donnan and McClelland 1999: 20 for a more detailed description of the Larco chronology. Castillo (2001: 308) suggested that the ceramic sequence in Jequetepeque is better described in three phases: Early Moche (corresponding to Larco's Phases I and II), Middle Moche (Phase III and part of Phase IV), and Late Moche (end of Phase IV and Phase V). He suggested further that Late Moche at Moro can be divided into three subphases.

12 There has been, however, some difficulty differentiating between Phase I and Phase II; thus, they are often combined into Phase I–II (Donnan and McClelland 1999: 21).

13 Although a few fineline painted ceramics have been found at San José de Moro that are attributed to Middle Moche, this volume focuses on the fineline painted ceramics that were produced there during Late Moche.

14 We found a few sherds of painted vessels at Moro on the surface and in fill.

CHAPTER 2   MORO-STYLE PAINTED VESSELS

1 The tombs we excavated also contained Huari vessels, as well as vessels brought from distant cultures, such as Cajamarca and Nieveria; however, we will not describe those vessels in this volume.

2 Some Phase IV ceramic vessels from the Southern Moche Region have horizontal tubes through their chambers (Purin 1980: Pl. XLVI; Donnan and McClelland 1999: Fig. 4.55). Chambers with tubes can also be found in much earlier ceramics. A spouted bottle attributed to "Late Chavín" has two intersecting tubes across the middle of the chamber (Lapiner 1976: Fig. 96 and Note 96, p. 438).

3 Compare figure 2.2d.

4 A vessel with a similar chamber form but with a stirrup spout was reported from the Lambayeque Valley, three valleys north of Moro, by Shimada (1994: 245). It was decorated with painted spiders and came from a flexed burial at Huaca Lucia, Batan Grande.

5 This bottle was archaeologically excavated. Looters probably discard many poor-quality vessels, thus skewing our impression of the overall quality of the fineline paintings.

6 Donnan and McClelland 1999: 84. Three-color Moro paintings are in the traditional Moche fineline painting style, except for the addition of a third color. They should not be confused with the Huari-derived polychrome painting style, which is discussed later in this chapter.

7 Weapon bundles consist of the weapons and sometimes the clothing of defeated opponents. The weapons may include a club, a shield, spears or darts, and a sling. Often, only a club and shield are shown. See The Warrior Narrative (p. 114) and Donnan and McClelland 1999: 60.

8 The relative frequency of decoration patterns is based only on bottles that appear to have their original spouts.

9 Castillo's continuing stratigraphic excavations have enabled him to determine that Phase V Moche fineline painting and Huari-influenced vessel forms and polychrome painting were introduced at about the same time at Moro (Castillo 2000, 2001).

10 For a more complete discussion of this process, see Donnan and McClelland 1999: 156–157.

CHAPTER 3   SUBJECT MATTER

1 This description of Moche subject matter during Phases I through IV applies only to the Southern Moche Region and not to Moro, since there was no extensive fineline painting tradition at Moro during those phases. For a detailed analysis of the Phase IV–V maritime shift, see McClelland 1990: 75–106.

2 About ninety paintings (35 percent of our Moro sample) contain boats. In comparison, we have identified only twelve paintings with boats (5 percent) in our sample from the Southern Moche Region during Phase V.

3 Donnan and McClelland 1999: Figs. 3.45, 4.42, 4.45, 4.72.

4 These objects are referred to as "net decks" because they support the occupant of the boat. They may actually be large nets that are packed around and on top of the cargo, providing a surface on which to sit.

5 Some boats from the Southern Moche Region carry more figures and feature fishing for a supernatural fish, an activity that has not been found in Moro boat paintings.

6 If this vessel had not been archaeologically excavated at Moro, its Moro attribution could be questioned. Although the vessel form is clearly Moro-style, there are some anomalies in the fineline style. To show the female holding the paddle, the artist had to turn her upper torso to a frontal position. Her legs appear to be tucked under her and she sits erect instead of leaning forward. She has only two snake tailings hanging down her back and no tiered train. Paddler and his boat are typical of Moro painting.

7 Wrinkle Face and Iguana are important supernatural creatures in Moche art. They are usually portrayed as companions who participate in a wide range of activities. Wrinkle Face is a fanged human figure who wears a feline headdress and a serpent-headed belt. He is usually, but not always, shown with distinct wrinkles on his face. Iguana combines human and iguana attributes and wears a bird headdress.

8 This type of boat was first identified by Cordy-Collins (1977: 421–434).

9 The Crested Animal appears in every Moche phase; however, these are the only Phase V examples of the Crested Animal from either Moro or the Southern Moche Region. See Donnan and McClelland (1999: 192) for two Phase I–II examples. The Crested Animal continues into at least middle Chimú, when two Crested Animals were rendered in low relief on a middle Chimú vessel (Donnan and Mackey 1978: Pl. 14).

10 Until a few decades ago, iguanas could be seen in the northern valleys.

11 Matthew Enger (personal communication).

12 During Phase IV in the Southern Moche Region, Wrinkle Face and Iguana participated in depictions of the Bean and Stick Ceremony. Other participants included supernatural humans and anthropomorphized felines, foxes, deer, and birds (Donnan and McClelland 1999: 114). Anthropomorphized beans were portrayed holding sets of sticks (Ibid.: 246).

13 In earlier Moche depictions of the Bean and Stick Ceremony, the participants are usually seated on the ground or amid sand hills.

14 A vessel of this type was first described by Rowe (1942), who referred to it as the De Vault specimen because it was in the collection of Dr. V. T. De Vault [3.80]. It was reportedly excavated from Sullana on the Chira River. Similarly shaped polychrome double spout and bridge bottles are often called De Vault bottles.

15 The vessel shown in figure 3.90 was excavated by Stumer at the site of Huaquerones in the Rimac Valley. He recognized the Bean and Stick Theme as a Moche design on a Huari-style double spout and bridge bottle (Stumer 1958: Fig. 5).

16 This enigmatic activity received its name because of the resemblance of the flowerlike objects to badminton shuttlecocks.

17 At the Pyramids in the Moche Valley, a male was buried with a long wooden spear, sheathed in copper, with copper crosspieces resembling those in the Ceremonial Badminton depictions (Donnan 1985).

18 De Bock (1998) referred to this theme as the Waterlily Ritual. He suggested that the flowerlike objects are water lilies attached to weighted cords.

19 Runner scenes are more common in the Southern Moche Region during Phase V. Our sample contains ten runner scenes out of about 250 Phase V vessels from that area. Both human and animal runners are shown, and the humans wear the "runner's uniform."

20 Donnan and McClelland 1999: Fig. 2.18.

21 Donnan and McClelland 1999: 130.

22 Donnan and McClelland 1999: Fig. 4.106.

23 Donnan and McClelland 1979.

24 For more information on the Burial Theme and its layout, see Donnan and McClelland 1979, 1999: 166.

25 It may represent an animal to be buried in the tomb.

26 Burial and Assembly are painted on the chamber first, sometimes restricting the space available for the Conch Shell Transfer and Sacrifice sections. The painting sequence is illustrated in Donnan and McClelland 1999: 166–167.

27 Donnan 1972.

28 Donnan and McClelland 1999: 130.

29 Quilter (1997) wrote a detailed interpretation of this scene.

30 During Phase IV, artists began to animate nonliving objects by attaching human arms and legs to them (Donnan and McClelland 1999: 113). Often these animated objects fight or capture human warriors (Quilter 1990).

31 Goblets are intrinsic elements in the Sacrifice Ceremony.

32 The spiral in this illustration is broken into six rows to facilitate display. Except for the topmost figure, the break points were selected to equalize the row length and have no other significance. For a view of the drawing laid out in a continuous row, see Donnan and McClelland 1999: Fig. 5.45. For a detailed description of this vessel, see Donnan 1981.

33 In this discussion, animals include sea animals of all types, terrestrial animals, birds, insects, and arachnids. Natural animals have no features other than those that would be found on the animal in nature. Anthropomorphized animals have some attributes of natural or supernatural humans, such as human arms, legs, head, clothing, ornaments, weapons, or musical instruments. Zoomorphized animals are those comprising parts of more than one animal, but no human parts.

34 About 15 percent of our Moro sample features natural and anthropomorphized animals and other creatures in ocean settings. See also McClelland 1990.

35 In earlier Moche phases, crabs had a variety of carapace shapes. Many crabs with carapaces similar to those illustrated by the Moche can be still be seen on the sandy beaches today.

36 Two stirrup spout vessels have modeled frogs placed near the openings of the tubes passing through their chambers [3.107, 3.134].

37 Perhaps they are leftover fish dinners of the sea lions.

38 These stones are still used by shamans (Donnan 1978: 136). A hunting scene showing these stones is illustrated in Donnan and McClelland 1999: Fig. 4.87. Clubbing the sea lions can cause them to cough up the digestive stones.

39 At least five species of flying fish are found along the coast of Peru (Love et al. 2005). They swim rapidly close to the surface and launch themselves into the air to escape predators, gliding at up to 60 km/h on outstretched elongated pectoral fins. Their flights typically extend 30 to 50 m. They can reinitiate their glide and prolong their flight by lowering their forked tails (caudal fins) into the water and lashing them rapidly like miniature outboard motors (Oceanlink 2006, Wikipedia 2006).

40 These colorful shells come from deep, warm water off the coast of Ecuador. They do not grow in the cold coastal waters of Peru. Only a few whole *Spondylus* shells have been reported from Moche sites. Moche metal workers had access to the colorful shells — they used them as inlays in elegant jewelry.

41 Compare this Moro depiction with a Phase IV painting of a splayed owl (Donnan and McClelland 1999: Fig. 4.46).

42 Since the female almost always wears a net "dress" and sits on a net platform in a reed boat, the netting could be associated with the web weavings of spiders. The association of the female with spiders can be traced back to a Phase IV painting. The female sits in her crescent boat above anthropomorphized spiders, which hold a ladder for the Warrior Priest to climb (Donnan and McClelland 1999: Fig. 4.27).

43 Murphy 1925: 244.

44 Goblets are associated with the Sacrifice Ceremony (Donnan and McClelland 1999: 130).

45 McClelland 1977.

46 The remains of ulluchu fruit have been archaeologically excavated in funerary settings at Sipán (Alva 1994: 184) and Dos Cabezas (Donnan n.d.). The very fragile, desiccated specimens are less than three centimeters long. In spite of efforts by several investigators, the ulluchu has not yet been botanically identified.

47 Approximately 20 percent of vessels and sherds in our Phase V sample from the Southern Moche Region are decorated with geometric designs. The actual fraction of all southern Phase V fineline vessels represented by geometric paintings is probably much higher.

48 Donnan 1973: Pl. 7E.

49 Patricia Knobloch (personal communication) has indicated that students of Huari art use the term "rays" to describe similar objects; however, we have used that term to describe different objects, such as the lines emanating from the female in crescent boat scenes. The precedent for the volute is clearly seen in Huari ceramics (Lavalle 1984: 120, 139). The volute design continues into early Chimú jars in the Moche Valley (Donnan and Mackey 1978: Pl. 12).

50 Castillo excavated the vessel in figure 3.178 in a cache (personal communication).

51 Castillo excavated the vessel in figure 3.182 in a Moche burial (personal communication).

52 Donnan (1973: Pl. 7A–D) reported a cache in the Santa Valley containing two pairs of pod-shaped vessels similar in form and design to the two Moro pieces.

CHAPTER 4 THE MORO ARTISTS

1 For a more detailed description of our methods of identifying and naming individual Moche artists, see Donnan and McClelland 1999: 187–190.

2 See Donnan and McClelland (1999: 269–283) for a discussion of the six original Moro artists and the features that characterize their works. Their paintings are not repeated here as a group, although they are included in the present volume under the various subject matter headings. In each case, the artist is indicated in the figure caption.

3 Donnan and McClelland 1999: 172.

4 Modeled frogs cling to the double stirrup arches of both vessels. Although the upper spout of one vessel is broken off, it probably resembled the other one, with two frontal figures holding manioc between corn stalks.

CHAPTER 5 CONCLUSIONS

1 Foreign ceramics that have been excavated in the Late Moche tombs at Moro include the Nieveria style from the Central Coast and the Cajamarca style from the Northern Moche Region. However, there is no evidence that Moche artists at Moro copied or were influenced by these styles.

2 Donnan and McClelland 1999: 172.

3 McClelland 1997.

4 Donnan 1973: Pl. 7E.

5 Donnan 1972.

6 Rowe 1942.

7 Stumer 1958.

8 For a more detailed discussion of post-Moche artistic traditions, see Donnan and McClelland 1999: 184–185.

9 Lavalle 1989: 201, 211, 219.

10 Lavalle 1989: 70, 223.

References Cited

Alva, Walter
1994   Sipán. *Colección Cultura y Artes del Perú*. Edited by José Antonio de Lavalle. Cervecería Backus & Johnston del Perú, Lima.

Castillo B., Luis Jaime
2000   Huari y Tiwanaku: Modelos vs. Evidencias. In *Boletín de Arqueología PUCP, Primera parte*. Edited by Peter Kaulicke and William H. Isbell, pp. 143–180. Lima.
2001   The Last of the Mochicas: A View from the Jequetepeque Valley. In *Moche Art and Archaeology in Ancient Peru, Studies in the History of Art 63*. Edited by Joanne Pillsbury, pp. 306–332. Center for Advanced Study of the Visual Arts, Symposium Papers XL. National Gallery of Art, Washington, D.C.

Castillo B., Luis Jaime and Christopher B. Donnan
1994   La Ocupación Moche de San José de Moro, Jequetepeque. In *Moche: Propuestas y Perspectivas*. Edited by Santiago Uceda and Elías Mujica, pp. 93–146. Universidad Nacional de La Libertad, Trujillo.

Chodoff, David
1979   Investigaciones Arqueológicas en San José de Moro. In *Arqueología Peruano*. Compiled by R. Matos Mendieta, pp. 37–47. Universidad Nacional Mayor de San Marcos y Comisión para Intercambio Educativo entre los Estados Unidos y el Perú, Lima.

Cock, Guillermo Alberto
1985   *From the Powerful to the Powerless: The Jequetepeque Valley Lords in the 16th Century, Peru*. Master's thesis, Department of Anthropology, University of California, Los Angeles.

Cordy-Collins Alana
1977   The Moon Is a Boat!: A Study in Iconographic Methodology. In *Pre-Columbian Art History: Selected Readings*. Edited by Alana Cordy-Collins and Jean Stern, pp. 421–434. Peek Publications, Palo Alto.

De Bock, Edward K.
1998   The Waterlily Ritual: An Andean Political and Religious Ceremony of the Moche Culture. *Journal of the Steward Anthropological Society* 26(1–2): 1–18.

Disselhoff, Hans Dietrich
1956   Tumbas de San José de Moro (Provincia de Pacasmayo, Perú). In *Proceedings of the 32nd International Congress of Americanists* (Copenhagen, 1956), pp. 364–367.
1957   Polychrome Keramik in der nord peruanischen Küstenzone. *Baessler-Archiv*, n.s., 5(2): 203–207. Museum für Völkerkunde, Berlin.
1958   Cajamarca-Keramik von der Pampa von San José de Moro, Provincia Pacasmayo. *Baessler-Archiv*, n.s. 6(1): 181–194. Museum für Völkerkunde, Berlin.

Donnan, Christopher B.
1972   Moche-Huari Murals from Northern Peru. *Archaeology* 25(2): 85–95.
1973   The Moche Occupation of the Santa Valley, Peru. *University of California Publications in Anthropology*, Vol. 8. Berkeley and Los Angeles.
1977   The Thematic Approach to Moche Iconography. In *Pre-Columbian Art History: Selected Readings*. Edited by Alana Cordy-Collins and Jean Stern, pp. 407–420. Peek Publications, Palo Alto.
1978   *Moche Art of Peru, Pre-Columbian Symbolic Communication*. Museum of Cultural History, University of California, Los Angeles.
1981   Moche V Bottle with Complex Fineline Drawing. In *The Shape of the Past: Studies in Honor of Franklin D. Murphy*. Edited by G. Buccellati and C. Speroni, pp. 55–64. Institute of Archaeology and Office of the Chancellor, University of California, Los Angeles.
1985   Archaeological Confirmation of a Moche Ceremony. *Indiana* (Berlin) 10: 371–381.
1990   Masterworks of Art Reveal a Remarkable Pre-Inca World. *National Geographic* 177(6): 16–33.
1997   Introduction. In *The Pacatnamú Papers Volume 2: The Moche Occupation*. Edited by Christopher B. Donnan and Guillermo A. Cock, pp. 9–16. Fowler Museum of Cultural History, University of California, Los Angeles.
2001   Moche Burials Uncovered. *National Geographic* 199(3): 58–73.
n.d.   *Moche Tombs at Dos Cabezas*. Unpublished manuscript, University of California, Los Angeles.

Donnan, Christopher B. and Carol J. Mackey
1978   *Ancient Burial Patterns of the Moche Valley, Peru*. University of Texas Press, Austin.

Donnan, Christopher B. and Donna McClelland
1979   *The Burial Theme in Moche Iconography*. Dumbarton Oaks, Washington, D.C.
1999   *Moche Fineline Painting: Its Evolution and Its Artists*. Fowler Museum of Cultural History, University of California, Los Angeles.

Kutscher, Gerdt
1983   *Nordperuanische Gefäßmalereinen des Moche-Stils*. Verlag C.H. Beck, Munich.

Lapiner, Alan
1976   *Pre-Columbian Art of South America*. Harry N. Abrams, New York.

Lavalle, José Antonio
1984   *Culturas Precolombinas, Huari*. Colección Arte y Tesoros del Peru, Banco de Crédito del Peru in La Cultura, Lima.
1988   *Culturas Precolombinas, Chimú*. Colección Arte y Tesoros del Peru, Banco de Crédito del Peru in La Cultura, Lima.
1989   *Culturas Precolombinas, Lambayeque*. Colección Arte y Tesoros del Peru, Banco de Crédito del Peru in La Cultura, Lima.

Love, Milton S., C. W. Mecklenbury, T. A. Mecklenbury, and L. K. Thorsteinson
2005   Resource Inventory of Marine and Estuarine Fishes of the West Coast and Alaska: A Checklist of North Pacific and Arctic Ocean Species from Baja California to the Alaska-Yukon Border. OCS Study MMS 2005-030 and USGS/NBII 2005-001. Seattle: U.S. Department of the Interior, U.S. Geological Survey, Biological Resources Division.

McClelland, Donna
1977   The Ulluchu: A Moche Symbolic Fruit. In *Pre-Columbian Art History, Selected Readings*. Edited by Alana Cordy-Collins and Jean Stern, pp. 435–452. Peek Publications, Palo Alto.
1990   A Maritime Passage from Moche to Chimu. In *The Northern Dynasties: Kingship and Statecraft in Chimor*. Edited by Michael Edward Moseley and Alana Cordy-Collins, pp. 75–106. Dumbarton Oaks, Washington, D.C.
1997   Moche Fineline Ceramics at Pacatnamú. In *The Pacatnamú Papers Volume 2: The Moche Occupation*. Edited by Christopher B. Donnan and Guillermo A. Cock, pp. 265–282. Fowler Museum of Cultural History, University of California, Los Angeles.

Murphy, Robert Cushman
1925   *Bird Islands of Peru: The Record of a Sojourn on the West Coast*. G.P. Putnam's Sons, New York.

Narvaez V., Alfredo
1994   La Mina: Una Tumba Moche I en el Valle de Jequetepeque. In *Moche: Propuestas y Perspectivas*. Edited by Santiago Uceda and Elías Mujica, pp. 59–92. Universidad Nacional de La Libertad, Trujillo.

Oceanlink
2006   oceanlink.island.net/oinfo/biodiversity/flyingfish/flyingfish.html. Accessed October 30, 2006.

Purin, Sergio
1980   *Vases Mochicas des Musées Royaux d'Art et d'Histoire, Fascicule II*. Corpus Antiquitatum Americanensium Union Academique Internationale, Belgique, Brussels.

Quilter, Jeffrey
1990   The Moche Revolt of the Objects. *Latin American Antiquity* 1(1): 42–65.
1997   The Narrative Approach to Moche Iconography. *Latin American Antiquity* 8(2): 113–133. Society for American Archaeology, Washington, D.C.

Rowe, John Howland
1942   A New Pottery Style from the Department of Piura, Peru. In
        Notes on Middle American Archaeology and Ethnology. Carnegie
        Institute of Washington, Division of Historical Research,
        Washington, D.C.

Shimada, Izumi
1994   *Pampa Grande and the Mochica Culture.* University of Texas
        Press, Austin.

Stumer, Louis M.
1958   Contactos Foráneos en la Arquitectura de la Costa Central.
        Lima: *Revista del Museo Nacional* 27: 11–30.

Wikipedia
2006   en.wikipedia.org/wiki/Flyingfish. Accessed October 30,
        2006.

Sources of Illustrations

Unless otherwise noted, rollout drawings are by Donna McClelland, photographs of ceramic vessels are by Christopher B. Donnan, and maps and other photographs are by Donald McClelland. We are grateful to the institutions and collections listed herein for their courtesy in enabling us to illustrate their vessels.

Numbers in square brackets are confidence values (see p. 7).

1.4a See figure 3.124
1.4b See figure 3.114
1.7a Proyecto Arqueológico San José de Moro [1]
1.7b See figure 4.2
1.7c See figure 4.11
2.1a See figure 3.125
2.1b Private collection [not from Moro]
2.2a Museo Arqueológico Rafael Larco Herrera, Lima [5]
2.2b Private collection [4]
2.2c Museo Arqueológico Rafael Larco Herrera, Lima [5]
2.2d See figure 3.144
2.3a See figure 3.134
2.3b See figure 3.154
2.4a Private collection [2]
2.4b See figure 3.112
2.4c See figure 3.119
2.5a See figure 3.29
2.5b See figure 3.35
2.5c See figure 3.131
2.5d See figure 3.76
2.5e See figure 3.94 and 4.23
2.5f See figure 3.8
2.5g See figure 3.155C
2.5h See figure 3.177
2.6 See figure 3.123
2.7 See figure 4.15
2.8 See figure 3.42
2.9a See figure 3.145
2.9b See figure 3.143

2.10 Proyecto Arqueológico San José de Moro [1]
2.11 See figure 4.22
2.12a See figure 3.156
2.12b Proyecto Arqueológico San José de Moro [1]
2.12c See figure 3.174
2.12d See figure 3.181
2.12e Proyecto Arqueológico San José de Moro [1]
2.13a See figure 3.181
2.13b See figure 3.163
2.13c See figure 3.156
2.13d See figure 3.172
2.13e See figure 3.179
2.13f See figure 34.21
2.14a Proyecto Arqueológico San José de Moro [1]
2.14b See figure 3.182
2.14c Private collection [4]
2.15a Museo Nacional de Antropología, Arqueología y Historia, Lima [not from Moro]
2.15b Museo Nacional de Antropología, Arqueología y Historia, Lima [not from Moro]
2.15c See figure 3.125
2.16a Proyecto Arqueológico San José de Moro [1]
2.16b Private collection [5]
2.17a Private collection [4]
2.17b Museo Arqueológico Rafael Larco Herrera, Lima [5]
2.18 See figure 3.48b
2.19 Private collection [4]
2.20a See figure 3.12
2.20b See figure 3.107
2.20c See figure 3.16
2.20d See figure 3.1
2.20e See figure 3.105
2.20f See figure 3.115
2.20g See figure 3.132
2.20h See figure 3.101
2.20i See figure 3.50
2.20j See figure 3.111
2.21a See figure 3.107
2.21b See figure 3.91
2.22a See figure 3.29
2.22b See figure 4.6
2.22c See figure 3.144
2.22d See figure 3.128
2.22e See figure 3.134
2.22f See figure 3.12
2.22g Private collection [5]
2.22h See figure 3.94
2.23 Private collection [2]
2.24 Proyecto Arqueológico San José de Moro [1]
3.1 Private collection [2]

3.3a Museo Nacional de Antropología, Arqueología y Historia, Lima [not from Moro]
3.4 Musées Royaux d'Art et d'Histoire, Brussels. Drawing by Edward De Bock [2]
3.5 Private collection [2]
3.6 Private collection [5]
3.7 Proyecto Arqueológico San José de Moro [1]
3.8 Museo Amano, Lima [2]
3.9 Fowler Museum at UCLA, Los Angeles [2]
3.10 Private collection [5]
3.11 Fowler Museum at UCLA, Los Angeles [2]
3.12 Private collection [5]
3.13 Private collection [2]
3.14 Private collection [2]
3.15 Museo de América, Madrid [5]
3.16 Private collection [5]
3.17 Private collection [4]
3.18 Staatliches Museum für Völkerkunde, Munich [5]
3.19 Private collection [5]
3.20 Private collection [5]
3.21 Proyecto Arqueológico El Brujo [5]
3.22 Private collection [4]
3.23a Proyecto Arqueológico San José de Moro [1]
3.23b Museo de la Nación, Lima [2]
3.24 Museo de la Nación, Lima [2]
3.25 Private collection [2]
3.26 Museo Arqueológico Rafael Larco Herrera, Lima [2]
3.27 Proyecto Arqueológico San José de Moro [1]
3.28 Private collection [4]
3.29 Proyecto Arqueológico San José de Moro [1]
3.30 Private collection [2]
3.31 Private collection [2]
3.32 Museo de la Nación, Lima [5]
3.33 Private collection [2]
3.34 Museo Prehistorico Ethnographico Luigi Pigorini [5]
3.35 Private collection [5]
3.36 Private collection [2]
3.37 Private collection [5]
3.38 Museo Arqueológico Rafael Larco Herrera, Lima [5]
3.39 Museo Amano, Lima [5]
3.40 Museo de la Nación, Lima [4]
3.41 Museo de la Nación, Lima [4]
3.42 Instituto Nacional de Cultura, Trujillo, Peru [5]
3.43 Museo Arqueológico Rafael Larco Herrera, Lima [5]
3.44 Private collection [2]
3.45 Proyecto Arqueológico San José de Moro [1]

3.48a Museo de Arqueológio de la Universidad de Trujillo [2]
3.48b Proyecto Arqueológico San José de Moro [1]
3.49 Private collection [2]
3.50 Proyecto Arqueológico San José de Moro [1]
3.51 Private collection [4]
3.52 Private collection [2]
3.53 Fowler Museum at UCLA, Los Angeles [2]
3.54 Private collection [2]
3.55 Fowler Museum at UCLA, Los Angeles [2]
3.56 Private collection [2]
3.58a See figure 4.17
3.58b See figure 4.15
3.59 Museo Amano, Lima [2]
3.60 Proyecto Arqueológico San José de Moro [1]
3.61 Private collection [2]
3.62 Private collection [4]
3.63 Museo Nacional de Antropología, Arqueología y Historia, Lima [5]
3.64 Proyecto Arqueológico San José de Moro [1]
3.65 Private collection [2]
3.66 University Museum of Archaeology and Anthropology, University of Pennsylvania, Philadelphia. Drawing after Kutscher 1983: 266 [2]
3.67 Proyecto Arqueológico San José de Moro [1]
3.68 Museo Chileno de Arte Precolombino, Santiago [2]
3.69 Museo Nacional de Antropología, Arqueología y Historia, Lima [2]
3.70 Private collection [5]
3.71 Private collection [5]
3.72 Fowler Museum at UCLA, Los Angeles [2]
3.73 Private collection [2]
3.74 Proyecto Arqueológico San José de Moro [1]
3.75 Proyecto Arqueológico San José de Moro [1]
3.76 Private collection [2]
3.77 Private collection [2]
3.78 Private collection [2]
3.79 Private collection [2]
3.80 Museo de la Nación, Lima [5]
3.81 Private collection [5]
3.82 Private collection [2]
3.83 Museo Arqueológico Rafael Larco Herrera, Lima [2]
3.84 Museo de Arqueológio de la Universidad de Trujillo [2]
3.85 Private collection [2]
3.86 Private collection [2]
3.87 Museo Nacional de Antropología, Arqueología y Historia, Lima [2]

3.88 Museo Arqueológico Rafael Larco Herrera, Lima [2]
3.89 Museo Arqueológico Rafael Larco Herrera, Lima [5]
3.90 Stumer 1958 [5]
3.91 Private collection [3]
3.92 Fowler Museum at UCLA, Los Angeles [5]
3.93 Proyecto Arqueológico San José de Moro [1]
3.94 Private collection [5]
3.95 Proyecto Arqueológico San José de Moro [1]
3.96 Private collection [2]
3.97 Private collection [2]
3.99 Museo Cassinelli, Trujillo [5]
3.101 Proyecto Arqueológico San José de Moro [1]
3.103 Proyecto Arqueológico San José de Moro [1]
3.104 Private collection [not from Moro]
3.105 Fowler Museum at UCLA, Los Angeles [2]
3.106 Donnan 1972 [5]
3.107 Fowler Museum at UCLA, Los Angeles [2]
3.108 Private collection [2]
3.109 Fowler Museum at UCLA, Los Angeles [2]
3.110 Private collection [2]
3.111 Private collection [2]
3.112 Museo Chileno de Arte Precolombino, Santiago [2]
3.113 Museo Nacional de Antropología, Arqueología y Historia, Lima [5]
3.114 Museum of Art, Rhode Island School of Design, Providence [5]
3.115 Private collection [5]
3.116 Private collection [2]
3.117 Private collection [2]
3.118 Private collection [5]
3.119 Private collection [2]
3.120 Proyecto Arqueológico San José de Moro [1]
3.121 Museum für Völkerkunde, Berlin [5]
3.122 Private collection [4]
3.123 Private collection [2]
3.124 GRASSI Museum für Völkerkunde zu Leipzig [5]
3.125 Private collection [2]
3.126 Private collection [2]
3.127 Private collection [2]
3.128 Fowler Museum at UCLA, Los Angeles [2]
3.129 Private collection [2]
3.130 Private collection [2]
3.131 Museum voor Volkenkunde, Rotterdam. Drawing by Edward De Bock [2]
3.132 Proyecto Arqueológico San José de Moro [1]
3.133 Private collection [2]
3.134 Museo de la Nación, Lima [5]

3.135 Private collection [5]
3.136 Private collection [2]
3.137a Private collection [2]
3.137b Private collection [2]
3.137c Private collection [2]
3.138 Private collection [2]
3.139 Private collection [2]
3.140 Private collection [2]
3.141 Private collection [2]
3.142 Proyecto Arqueológico San José de Moro [1]
3.143 Proyecto Arqueológico San José de Moro [1]
3.144 Private collection [2]
3.145 Proyecto Arqueológico San José de Moro [1]
3.146 Baltimore Museum of Art (photographs courtesy of Baltimore Museum of Art) [5]
3.147 Private collection [5]
3.148 Private collection [2]
3.149 Private collection [2]
3.150 Museo de la Nación, Lima [2]
3.153 Private collection [5]
3.154 Proyecto Arqueológico San José de Moro [1]
3.155a Museo de la Nación, Lima [2]
3.155b Private collection [2]
3.155c Private collection [5]
3.156 Private collection [2]
3.157 Museo Amano, Lima [5]
3.158 Private collection [2]
3.159 Private collection [4]
3.160 Proyecto Arqueológico San José de Moro [1]
3.161 Private collection [2]
3.162 Private collection [2]
3.163 Fowler Museum at UCLA, Los Angeles [2]
3.167 Private collection [2]
3.168 Museo Arqueológico "Horacio H. Urteaga", Cajamarca [2]
3.169a Proyecto Arqueológico San José de Moro [1]
3.169b Museo Nacional de Antropología, Arqueología y Historia, Lima [5]
3.170 Proyecto Arqueológico San José de Moro [1]
3.171 Private collection [2]
3.172 Private collection [2]
3.173 Proyecto Arqueológico San José de Moro [1]
3.174 Museo Arqueológico Rafael Larco Herrera, Lima [5]
3.175 Museo Arqueológico "Horacio H. Urteaga", Cajamarca [2]
3.176 Proyecto Arqueológico San José de Moro [1]
3.177 Private collection [2]
3.178 Proyecto Arqueológico San José de Moro [1]
3.179 Private collection [2]

3.180 Museo Arqueológico Rafael Larco Herrera, Lima [2]
3.181 Museo Arqueológico Rafael Larco Herrera, Lima [2]
3.182 Private collection [4]
3.183 Private collection [4]
4.1 Linden-Museum, Stuttgart [3]
4.2 Proyecto Arqueológico San José de Moro [1]
4.3 Private collection [3]
4.4 Museo Arqueológico Rafael Larco Herrera, Lima [3]
4.5 Museo Cassinelli, Trujillo [3]
4.6 Proyecto Arqueológico San José de Moro [1]
4.7 Museo Nacional de Antropología, Arqueología y Historia, Lima [3]
4.8 Private collection [3]
4.9 Proyecto Arqueológico San José de Moro [1]
4.10 Private collection [3]
4.11 Private collection [5]
4.12 Private collection [5]
4.13 Private collection [4]
4.14 Musée de l'Homme, Paris. Drawing after Kutscher 83: 315 [5]
4.15 Private collection [5]
4.16 Proyecto Arqueológico San José de Moro [1]
4.17 Proyecto Arqueológico San José de Moro [1]
4.18 Proyecto Arqueológico San José de Moro [1]
4.19 Proyecto Arqueológico San José de Moro [1]
4.20 Proyecto Arqueológico San José de Moro [1]
4.21 Proyecto Arqueológico San José de Moro [1]
4.22 Private collection [2]
4.23 Private collection [5]
4.24 Private collection [2]
4.25 Museo Arqueológico Rafael Larco Herrera, Lima [2]
4.26 Museo Arqueológico Rafael Larco Herrera, Lima [2]
4.27 Private collection [2]
4.28 Museo Arqueológico Rafael Larco Herrera, Lima [5]
4.29 Proyecto Arqueológico San José de Moro [1]
4.30 Proyecto Arqueológico San José de Moro [1]
4.31 Proyecto Arqueológico San José de Moro [1]
4.32 Private collection [3]
4.33 Private collection [3]
4.34 Proyecto Arqueológico San José de Moro [1]
5.1 Lavalle 1989: 211 [not from Moro]
5.2 Lavalle 1988: 75 [not from Moro]
5.3 Lavalle 1989: 23 [not from Moro]

Index